MARC BLANCHARD

Editor's Preface: Michel Leiris (1901–1990) in Perspective

Michel Leiris has been at the core of French letters since the publication of *L'Age d'homme* (*Manhood*) more than fifty years ago. It is also true, however, that Leiris has remained a lonely somewhat reserved figure on the sidelines of Surrealism, Existentialism, and even modern French poetry. He was only a distant companion to Breton and the Surrealists, more likely an observer of the *engagé* culture of the forties and fifties, while also very much, albeit in a different way from Bonnefoy or Char, a believer in the power of the poetic word. Perhaps his greatest title to minor fame is that he was with Caillois and Bataille, a member of the ephemeral Collège de Sociologie. But even in that enterprise, Leiris remained aloof. This distance from movements and people, from the fashions and the politics of the day may have given Leiris an aura. From Blanchot to Pontalis, to Lévinas, critics have recognized the unique place Leiris's work occupies in the literary tradition while they have also pointed out its exemplarity and its richness across disciplines: poetics, anthropology, psychoanalysis, and the history of art. For them Leiris generally represents an authoritative reference for any investigation combining literature and the human sciences in the field of daily life. In France, the new journal *Gradhiva* on the history of anthropological thought, edited by Jean Jamin with Leiris himself as the *génie tutélaire*, has confirmed Leiris's relevance to French intellectual history and ethnopoetics in particular. In the United States, the new school of cultural anthropology has shown interest in the long and happy conjunction of literary and anthropological interests in Leiris's work. But Leiris also paid the price of his radical difference. He wrote no manifestoes, he was part of no

YFS 81, *On Leiris,* ed. Blanchard, © 1992 by Yale University.

school and his only properly injunctive text, *L'Age d'homme,* published in the heydays of Surrealism, can still be read today as the first piece in the puzzle worked out in his interminable autobiographical enterprise, *La Règle du jeu.*

It is time to examine Leiris's perennial modernity and each of the pieces in this issue tries, in its own way, to account for Leiris's continuous presence on the French literary horizon between 1930 and the present. First Lydia Davis, whose translation of the first volume of *La Règle du jeu, Biffures,* has now been published, gives us a preview of her translation of the second volume, *Fourbis,* and she shares with us Leiris's linguistic and poetic challenge to all translators of his work. Jean-Christophe Bailly provides a reassessment of Leiris's *oeuvre* in the perspective of a generalized poetics. Francis Marmande looks at Leiris as the ultimate go-between in literature, the arts, and the human sciences. Denis Hollier retraces Leiris's archetypal autobiographical project. Leah Hewitt raises the question of *engagement* and Michèle Richman extends the political agenda to a Leirisian mythology of the sacred. Marc Blanchard speaks to protocols of literature and anthropology in Leiris's later books. Jean-Luc Nancy and Edouard Glissant express, each in his own way, their debt to a Leirisian poetic imagination. Finally, Emmanuel Lévinas, Maurice Blanchot, and J. B. Pontalis, whose earlier texts are reprinted here, tell us about the implications of the Leirisian project for a post-Mallarmean poetics in this our age of fragmentation and methodological despair.

Yale French Studies

On Leiris

Yale French Studies

Marc Blanchard, *Special editor for this issue*
Liliane Greene, *Managing editor*
Editorial board: Hillari Allred, Denis Hollier (Chair), Peter
   Brooks, Shoshana Felman, Christopher Miller, Kevin
   Newmark, Charles Porter, Amy Reid, Suzanne Toczyski
Staff: Cynthia Mesh
Editorial office: 82-90 Wall Street, Room 308.
Mailing address: 2504A-Yale Station, New Haven,
   Connecticut 06520.
Sales and subscription office:
   Yale University Press, 92A Yale Station
   New Haven, Connecticut 06520
   Published twice annually by Yale University Press

Designed by James J. Johnson and set in Trump Medieval
Roman by The Composing Room of Michigan, Inc.
Printed in the United States of America by the Vail Ballou
Press, Binghamton, N.Y.

ISSN 044–0078
ISBN for this issue 0–300–05707–5

LYDIA DAVIS

An Excerpt from *Fourbis*

TRANSLATOR'S NOTE

This passage is taken from a point very close to the beginning of Michel
Leiris's *Fourbis* (tentatively translated as *Flotsam*), the second volume
of his four-volume autobiographical work, *La Règle du jeu* [*The Rule of
the Game*]. His project in this, as in the first volume, *Biffures*
[*Crossouts*]—appeared last spring from Paragon House), and in a work
that preceded it and forms a sort of preface to it, *L'Age d'homme*
[*Manhood*], translated by Richard Howard and reissued recently by
North Point Press), is, in a sense, to write himself into existence, illustrating a reflection made by Michel Foucault: "Someone who is a
writer does not simply create an oeuvre in books . . . his principal
oeuvre is ultimately himself writing these books." Taking himself as
subject, with a sort of ethnographic objectivity, but expanding this
subjective terrain to include everything that impinges on and draws
out his words, he examines what is familiar, to him and often to us, so
closely and from such an odd angle that in the end it becomes strange,
an exotic close to home. Edmond Jabès has suggested about Leiris that
committed writing about the self ends in vulnerability before the
other. That is, if he is writing himself into existence, he needs the
cooperation of the reader for this.* What he shows us, too, is not only
the agony of extreme self-consciousness but also that to make a virtue
of a fault—to make a work of art out of a frank appraisal of one's
failings—does not alleviate the pain of these failings.

*This and some of the preceding references and formulations have been incorpo-
rated from James Clifford's excellent introductory remarks to the selection of Leiris's
work he edited for *Sulfur 15* (1986).

YFS 81, *On Leiris*, ed. Blanchard, © 1992 by Yale University.

The life of Michel Leiris—early surrealist, ethnographer, poet, novelist, and author of the many volumes of this ongoing auto-biographical opus—has not been an American or English life, and the language of that life, past and present, has not been English. Certain individual words, phrases, labels, titles, or remarks which fell upon his ears in French—from such oft-repeated family tags as *la maison d'en face* [the house across the street] to such subliminal childhood identifications as between *Mors, alphabet Morse, morse,* and *mors* [respectively a make of car, the Morse code, "walrus," and Latin for "death"]—have become, for him, knots where many threads of his remembrances and associations come together either tidily or untidily from every direction of his past and present. Though there is wordplay involved, often, these are not instances of conscious word-play for its own sake which a clever translator could approximately equal in her own language, but sounds of sentimental importance which must be retained in the original. This new, English text, then—not the "same" text as the one Michel Leiris wrote—must, because of the nature of his original, be tied back to that original with these same knots, so that the two texts are part of the same tangle. Thus, these words have been left in the original with English translation following in brackets.

Of course this shows up, yet again, the undeniable failure of any translation. The ideal translation would be, along the lines Borges laid out in his tale of Pierre Menard's *Don Quixote,* one in which every word would be matched by the same word in the same language but now not quite the same because written over again by a translator and, ideally, now understood by its readers, whatever their native language, so that the readers themselves would have been translated into a posi-tion to understand. And such a translation is, quite naturally, what the hard-pressed translator eventually comes to desire, in her striving for perfect equivalence, of both letter and spirit: there is always, at some point in her work, when she is faced with a difficulty that for a time defies solution, the sudden, spontaneous inclination to put down, as translation, the very same word or phrase she is staring at in the origi-nal text, perfect equivalent of itself though written anew, or reborn, in a new context. In the present text, in all awkwardness, readers have been given a cruder way, the way of imperfect translation as it must actually be, to "understand" the words that can only remain in the language their author wrote them in.

A second temptation, one degree away from the temptation to set the original down as translation of itself, is the temptation to translate into the closest possible, most literal English version of the text.

The French language is already, to begin with, a more formal language than the English language. Now, when a writer already writing in the formal language of French writes in a way that goes beyond this formality to a further, excessive, exaggerated formality, as Leiris does, the translator would like, ideally, to produce a version that is written in an English that is also excessively, exaggeratedly formal, and because Leiris's French is not only formal but also verbose, awkward, difficult (overloaded, precious, obscure, and containing such infelicities as mixed metaphors), as he himself admits with the honesty that is such an essential part of his project of self-examination, her English will ideally, in sum, be formal, verbose, awkward, and difficult to the same degree as the French away from what might be considered a more stylistically comfortable norm in each language—though her English should, ideally, never be quite as formal as his French since the languages are to different degrees formal to begin with. But the question of degree is what is difficult. She is immediately tempted, by the permission to write formally, verbosely, and awkwardly, to do what she must always have wanted to do, and that is to produce a translation so extremely close to the French original that it departs only far enough, not to be happy and comfortable English, but to be grammatically correct and coherent. There is great joy in this, both because it is something like an acrobatic trick or the solution to a clear mathematical problem, and because it is what she has always, in her translations, had to fight against doing. But the joy in the act blinds her only so long to the results—stilted and joyless reading. And so, with a sense of betrayal, now, though betrayal of what, she is not sure, she goes back into the translation and as gently as possible moves pieces and parts of it away from the literal, close parallel to the French and farther toward a more natural or at least happier English, though even this English may in the end be a sort of interlanguage, a limbo language: it is hard for her to tell because she has, by now, lost a good deal of familiar perspective, moving about more than ever before, as she herself is, in the limbo between languages which George Steiner suggests is the proper home of translations, a place she sees floating above the Atlantic and always heading toward the coast of Flanders or Normandy.

*   *   *   *

At Viroflay once again (and no doubt my age when I was taken there on vacation, four and then five, explains why that locality was the scene of so many of the experiences I am describing) I hear a high-pitched, apparently distant noise. A noise I am afraid of, because it is evening and dark on the road where we are walking. I don't think there were any of those trees there that were always so frightening when we turned at nightfall into an avenue or any sort of path bordered by them. No memory of foliage over my head or of one of those strange King of the Alder silhouettes so often traced by branches and trunks; rather, the open sky and perhaps even some stars. The noise that makes such a deep impression on me is a sort of rapid and continuous rattling, surely an insect's buzzing (but at that time I am incapable of such an identification). Do I look as though I am going to cry or do I seem *"tout chose"* [upset], my throat a little tight as I ask what sort of thing I'm hearing? My father says, to reassure me: "It's a car which is very far away, very far away," which makes me even more afraid.

Why not have said it was an insect? I think about it now and it awakens in me a little suspicion as to the veracity of the story. Perhaps I am distorting the quality of that noise when I describe a rasping comparable to the song of the cicada or the cricket, for it is doubtful that my father wouldn't have recognized this rasping, and the hypothesis of a misapprehension on his part being thus ruled out, what motive could have impelled him to talk to me about a car instead of quite simply ascribing to its real source a noise which, in order not to worry me, only had to be *explained* and would not have signified anything more alarming if caused by an insect's wing sheathes rather than a vehicle? Or have I taken this answer which my father is supposed to have given me and either changed it or coupled it with circumstances different from those in which he could actually have said something of that sort? Yet it seems to me that if my fear increased, it was in fact because of that explanatory phrase and its inadequacy, as though I had detected its falseness and thought it was only a white lie meant to *hide* something from me that I might have feared with good reason.

Whether or not this is a serious reason for rejecting my suspicion, it is still true that I have retained a very vivid memory of that fear. An imprecise, even fantastic memory of how my father might have been involved. A real memory of the fear provoked by that slight buzzing heard in the night, a noise the anguish of which resulted perhaps exclusively from the fact that it manifested the state of wakefulness of something infinitesimal or distant, the only sound present in the silence of a more or less country place where I imagined that at such an hour everything had to be asleep or beginning to fall asleep.

Fear of the night. Fear of the dark. But it is not only the impossibility of seeing or of seeing more than a compact mass of blackness that is involved. There is the idea of that opaque portion of time over which sleep reigns. A mysterious world, this, whose strangeness is felt when, awake oneself, one feels that others only live, now, with a reduced life, which in the adult can give rise to a certain euphoria but will be unpleasantly disturbing to the wakeful one if he is a child, ordinarily the first to bed and already unconscious while the grownups are still busy with their occupations. To take a walk on a summer evening, at the hour known as *entre chien et loup* [dusk; *lit.* between dog and wolf] (the border of day and night and also the frontier zone between the world of waking and the world of sleep) in a suburb still fairly rural some forty-five years ago was, of course, to a child as quick to feel uneasy as I always was, not a very reassuring thing. First of all, the twilight, a time of day that inclines one to dread (I noted this even when I was a grown man, when I came back from my first trip to Africa and had a certain difficulty reaccustoming myself to the Parisian twilights which, unlike the almost nonexistent twilight of the tropical regions, were intolerable to me, so long and sad did I find them). Then, the exoticism assumed, in the eyes of the young city-dweller I was, by a landscape which, though only a suburban one, was nevertheless more pastoral in appearance than the city setting I was used to. Lastly, the fact that as night approached even the immediate vicinity of a parish like Viroflay was deserted enough to create an impression of isolation in a child used to a certain life in the streets, even in the neighborhood, extremely quiet at that time, where his parents lived. There was reason to suppose, consequently, that before hearing the noise that intrigued me so strongly, I felt ill at ease, already prey to a vague fear that only required the slightest pretext to become concrete. What exactly, then, did that noise contribute?

I must answer this question if I want to reveal why such a story, more than any other I could call upon to illustrate the uneasiness with which the night inspired me, seems to me to sustain a particular relationship with the idea I have of death. But as I answer, I cannot avoid some constructing, since I will have to substitute reasoning and conjecture for what has been denied me by a memory too often defective, in my opinion. If, then, I fill a lacuna with this after-the-fact analysis and if, apparently reducing the excessively large portion of unknown that yawns in me, it seems to me I am at the same time diminishing the lion's share which the emptiness has carved out for itself there in anticipation, the portion of myself thus recaptured form nothingness will have been recaptured in a completely artificial and provisional way, without my being able to flatter myself that I have successfully concluded an enterprise that I would like to be able to compare to other filling operations like the great drainage labors performed in the seventeenth century by the Dutch to win habitable territories from the sea—labors I sometimes contemplate as images illustrating what art is, in the case of the works one can regard as its most important manifestations: an attempt to organize or colonize parcels of land which it is vitally important to protect from the nameless thing in us whose flood threatens us.

There is no sea—or Zuider Zee—around us, but only the country, or rather, what is to me country. Definitely, the noise of our footsteps on the road. A few lights, perhaps, scattered as the houses are scattered. It is likely that we are talking, that, father to mother, brother to brother (or sister), and parents to children we are exchanging desultory remarks about certain events of the day or small details along our path. A short after-dinner walk to help us digest our food and "take the air," since temporarily removing ourselves from the miasmas of Paris is the great aim of this summer sojourn. We must be, at the very most, a quarter of an hour from our house. My father must have arrived, as usual, by an evening train which, his work finished, he took from Saint Lazare Station. Suddenly, the noise.

If I hear cicadas in a sunny landscape, these days, it only carries to an extreme the pleasure I feel in finding myself bathed in light and heat: a festive din that would seem to have issued from a quantity of voices that are themselves only the expression, in another register, of an ardor and a luminosity too fierce to remain echoless. When, more than a year ago now, I heard the incredible racket produced in Martinique, as soon as darkness came, by the grasshoppers they call *"cabrit bois"* [wood goat] and the frogs—among other very diverse creatures customarily classified, all and sundry, as belonging to the animal kingdom—this too seemed comforting to me: no harmonic correspondence between this clamor and the moistness of a night in the rainy season in the tropics but, as in the case of the cicadas, a manifold jubilation and its musical result. In two different climates and at very different hours, a jumble of sounds, exuberance, a sonorous burgeoning signaling an incalculable number of presences, too infinitesimal to cause fear (as might an outburst from a human crowd) and, quite the contrary, reassuring since their number conjures up an intense life capable of proliferating to infinity.

Within the silence almost unbroken by our words and steps on the Viroflay road, what, then, did this noise—an insect's rasping or the thin engine sound of a car whose axles and spokes might be no more than frail dry limbs—what did this noise, in its uniqueness, come murmuring to me?

Having considered carefully, I think the noise said one single thing and that the unique thing that it said was that it was *unique*.

World of waking, world of sleep: quite distinct entities which, like two parallels, are meant to go along side by side but without ever meeting. We chatted and we walked, a family awake, in a place relatively deserted and wrapped in darkness. Only a few lights affirmed that not everything was absolutely asleep in this sea where we were a little island of wakefulness. A timid affirmation, without strength against the silence that testified all around to our isolation in the middle of an empty space, where no image of any living body loomed up and where no creature seemed even to attain a sufficient degree of reality for that reality, involving at least one instance of active functions breath, pulse, whatever?), to give birth to the least sound.

Because the motion of the day and the inertia of the night come together in him, a sleepwalker is always frightening. As was true of Jeannot, who, also in Viroflay, came one night to the foot of the bed of my cousin (the one who had such a marvellous railway in his garden) and said to him: "Come and play?" The noise I heard intruded, perhaps, into our little island in the manner of a sleepwalker slipping, all white in his nightshirt, through the shadows of a bedroom: an apparition proving that among all the things in sleep there is one—completely proximate to us though very distant from our world (for its gaze evokes nothing of what we find in the catalogue of human sentiments)—there is one that persists in carrying on its life, all alone and all closed in on itself. Quite as strange as a diver, prisoner of a costume that turns him into an amphibian, or as a Martian severed from his planet, is the advent of this upright stature before us, who though all the others were lying down, motionless between their sheets, and did not expect the coming of a spectre as alone among us as he would be in a cemetery. The same is the case with the intrusion of the isolated, unexpected voice (which is not even a voice). A weak song flung forth only for itself alone and which one divines to be the accompaniment or the direct product of some occupation which will not let itself be divined: a fragile sound which will not have carried any message through the labyrinth formed by the internal parts of the organ of hearing except to designate itself, too, an ambassador from the world of sleep (so neighbor to the world of death) since its high-pitched clinking introduced itself into our sphere of wakeful creatures as the unique sign of a unique obstinacy too solitary to be situated otherwise than *beyond*.

I am performing a series of shifts: from darkness to sleep, from suburb to desert, from oblivion to the Zuider Zee, from insect to sleepwalker, from solitude to death. With truly close associations of images or notions there mingles, here, a certain enthusiasm of the pen, always so quick to skip from one subject to another as soon as a severe censorship (a weighing of all the words) ceases to be exercised; and I hardly see why, at the pace I am going, I would restrain myself from calling upon *mandibules* [mandibles], for instance, to justify, with the help of the new link that arrives by the tortuous way of rhyme, passing from the insect to the *somnambule* [sleepwalker]—himself associated with that deep-sea worker, the diver, and then with the monster fallen from another planet—and thus strengthen the connection, a little too slack, that has already been established between the tardily susurrating little beast and the waking sleeper based on the idea of a *solitary from a strange world* (or *isolé insolite [peculiar isolate]*) *in nocturnal intrusion*. Doesn't *"mandibules"* [mandibles], more than *"gueule"* [mouth of an animal] or *"mâchoire"* [jaw of a person or animal] (so firmly situated in everyday life) harbor a singular danger, like the anthrax-carrying fly I thought I recognized in each of the fat buzzing flies whose brilliant, bluish black bodies were the color of anthracite?

If I return, now, to the very banal anecdote I have been mining this way, shaking it a bit to make it cough up and not resigning myself to setting it aside despite all that is dubious about it, I notice an omission: following the trail of the insect heard in the night, I ignored the car. Even if I am off the track when I attribute to my father the explanation of the noise by the distant presence of a vehicle (a vehicle drawn by an animal, and not an automobile, for *"voiture"* rolls along in me outfitted with that meaning, in this real memory or memory already in part mendacious and warped once again by the point of view of the here and now, which is that of a memory of a memory—a surprising false bottom! somewhat as there exists a theater of theater: the pantomime staged by Hamlet to unmask a guilty man who is himself only a king with a tinsel crown, or the silent scene unfolding in the background,

watched by a few of the actors placed on the proscenium and themselves watched by the public, so that those in the silent scene, second-
degree actors set in a distance accentuated by their muteness, pass
almost to the rank of apparitions, as is the case for my memory, elevated to the second power by the written recollection I make of it quite
aside from the fact that in itself it is already an unwarrantable interference of a noise faint enough and little enough localized so that one
may believe it has risen from the background of memory), even if such
an attribution is only an error that thrusts me into the unreality of
fiction, it remains true that at a certain moment of the time according
to which my life is made and unmade—a moment no doubt remote
since it was most likely earlier than the period when, in common
language, *"voiture"* began to be used to mean *"automobile"* (which, if
the moment in question had been later, would inevitably have produced in my thinking at least a little uncertainty about exactly how the
vehicle was moving along)—this carriage which could only be pulled
by a horse advanced toward me like one of those stage props contribut-
ing to produce an effect of fear, whether it may have been physically
part of the real scenario, or whether through some indiscernible af-
finity it may have added itself, one day, to the vague recollection which
was the more or less distorted reflection of that scenario.

The passage of a hackney carriage in the street, in the very depth of a
Paris night, when one has already been in bed for a certain length of
time. Nothing like the insect (for the shock of the hooves against the
pavement looses too thick a noise) and nothing even, really, like anything at all definite that one could pose as a parallel and that any sort of
analogy would allow to be introduced as a term of comparison. Unless
one were to summon up the diver at this point, with lead soles heavy
enough to be likened to horseshoes; but one hardly imagines a diver
capable of moving, once he has emerged from the depths, with such
agility that his step would have the merry aspect of a trot. The passage
of a hackney carriage, then, being neither insect nor diver; only a
hackney carriage pulled by a long-headed quadruped whose mouth, by
way of the bit, to which the reins are attached, is connected to the
hands of a cabman and whose flanks are caught between two shafts,
the sorts of shafts that break so often when the quadruped falls and
thrashes convulsively on the pavement, a sudden scandal because it is
a public explosion of tragedy, like the collapse of a person struck by
epilepsy or a person whose blood, all shame obliterated in the wake of
some accident, spreads out at once in a horrible excretion.

No notion, however, of violent death. The hackney cab, passing thus, is peaceful. Nice and rhythmical, it jogs quietly along. But what is it doing? And where is it going? Here things begin to go wrong, because one can't imagine an outing in a hackney cab at such an hour. No doubt it's going back to the stable? But that would be even more sinister. One pictures the straw, the hayrack, the weak light of the stable lamp, all this in a hovel in a poor neighborhood, within walls spotted with damp and on a floor choked with refuse. Too wretched a neighborhood for those who inhabit it to be true living beings. Creatures of another species, a species one doesn't know, that one only sees. The fear the middle-class child has of the drunk is really a fear of the *poor* drunk—of the poor man, quite simply, when he lets himself go at all, rejects the seemliness imposed on him by the order of well-to-do folk, and zigzags along the sidewalk or roadway bellowing like a true savage, thus showing that in fact he belongs to another species whose reactions, when they are no longer policed and he is on the loose, can only be formidable.

The passage of a hackney cab, at a meek trot, however, neither drunk nor revolutionary, a cab which could very well be, not a cab, but a barouche, if it weren't for that heavy step, which is not the step of a luxury horse (lighter and, as they say, more *"fringant"* [spirited]) but of a proletarian horse, a horse who has finished his day and whom his cabby, perhaps half-asleep, drives without a lash of the whip and without saying a word, to or from an unknown job which, having thus by definition become a mystery, worries us.

What is it doing? Where is it going? Insect, vehicle, or anything else at all, this is the question posed by the *isolé insolitement éveillé quand tout le reste est* (ou *paraît*) *endormi* [isolate oddly awake when all the others are (or seem) asleep]. We know nothing about what it really is and it exists for us only through the intrusion of its noise. Indifferent to everything, totally external to us (except that it insinuates itself through our ears), its activity is pursued. Perhaps its capacity, in the right circumstances, to provoke dread depends, even more than on the fact that its nature is so mysterious, on this simple, separate persistence, formal proof that—in the same way that we can be awake when others are asleep—something can be alive *without* us?

Something which, because of this fact, can only be heard by us as the sound of a knell: without anything in common with our own life (since this thing, whether we call it an insect or a horse-drawn carriage, remains fundamentally impenetrable given our ignorance of what it is occupied in doing), independent of us as it is independent of the others (of all those creatures who are, in appearance, asleep while it is awake), doesn't it express in a tangible way in imperturbable permanence which is the very permanence of the course of things, that is, one of the aspects of death the least easy to consider without trembling, namely, that our end will in all likelihood not be the end of the world but only an end limited—unjustly, it will always seem—to us?

"*Mors*" cars, once ranking among the fastest, their name evoking the soft and regular sound of the old electric automobiles (no engine in front, but a simple casing behind which one sees the liveried driver sitting straight up at his vertical wheel). The *alphabet Morse* [Morse code], which caused one to ask oneself if it hadn't some collusion with the signals from the planet Mars. The *morse* [walrus], an aquatic mammal of the same order as the seal (the juggling seal shown in circuses or the seal that dives with such a great splash into the zoo pool), very closely related, but perhaps fatter? and furnished with, besides the beautiful moustache of long stiff hairs planted in his muzzle, two great teeth jutting upward in the manner of tusks. *Mors*, death, as one will learn it when one studies Latin, when one will have forgotten the fear caused by the "*chauffeurs de la Drôme*" [Drôme scorchers], who are not *chauffeurs d'automobiles* [automobile drivers] masked in their goggles but brigands *chauffant* [heating] the feet of peasants to make them reveal where their money is hidden.

On the Picardy road, near Viroflay, there was also the "*Père l'Auto*" outdoor café: gardens and groves of trees, a gym set with rings, knotted rope, trapeze and swing, a game of *tonneau* [toad-in-the-hole], perhaps, but no game of *loto* [lotto]. At least once, I think, we drank lemonade there, unless it was a syrup of grenadine for me (a drink for which I substituted, several years later, *grenadine au kirsch* [grenadine with kirsch], a first step toward the frankly alcoholic beverages consumed by those for whom such slogans as "*La phtisie se prend sur le zinc*" [what you imbibe at the bar may be a case of consumption] and other prudent aphorisms have no validity). It seems to me, however, that associated with the imprecise and almost disembodied image that has remained with me of the "Père l'Auto" café is not the unctuousness of a syrupy drink, but the fizzing of lemonade—due to the bubbles visible in the glasses and even on the wood of the table, across the meniscus of each of the little pools formed by the small amount of liquid scattered almost inevitably at the moment of uncorking—so that, if it is clearly understood that not to mention grenadine (so plausible in such a place, in such a period, and at the age I was then) would indicate a lack of circumspection and, consequently, an error with respect to the scientific spirit from which I am absolutely determined not to depart, I am, at least, justified in mentioning it only secondarily.

I don't know if we went by way of that Picardy road, with its smell of tar, the day we visited *"Les Jardies,"* Gambetta's mortuary house, and returned home passing, it seems to me, by way of Jouy-en-Josas. What exactly is in that Jardies house? I've lost all memory of it. But there is definitely, at least, a bust and perhaps also some roses (unless here I am transforming a withering of immortelles or box into living flowers). Les Jardies—with rosery or without rosery, with the great man or without the great man in effigy—is, in any case, a curious name: it resembles *"jardin"* [garden] but does not have its freshness; it is damp, flat, emaciated, a little like the Picardy road.

In fact, what it designates is an oddity: a country house changed into a museum, immobilized—it and its outdoor settings—at a given point in time as though by a fairy's wand (so that, if there are roses in the garden, they are not present-day and natural roses but roses from the past which some artifice has endowed with perenniality); a place of habitation where a man lived and concerning which one no longer knows which of the many souvenirs one sees gathered there were things *of his* that surrounded him when he was alive, and which of them were only put there later, impersonal souvenirs of History and not repositories of a human memory. Gambetta roses, roses of the time of the visit to Les Jardies (which one is inclined to believe are the same and everlasting roses rather than roses seasonally renewed); and then the roses I am speaking of here, which are a memory of roses or roses I invent. The uncertainty in which I presume I was plunged as a child as to these roses blooming at the suture of two moments of duration, the prejudicial uncertainty which causes me here to use the term "presume" to *cover myself* (as they say in the language of the bureaucratised) in case of a possible accusation of frivolousness or even falsehood, leads me to approach obliquely one of the main cruxes of the question: the vertigo I feel as soon as I lose the thread of duration, as soon as I hesitate, too, between recollection and invention—like the vertigo I am yielding to at present and which is reaching its highest pitch, as though the motion by which one tries to contract time and resuscitate what was once experienced (a motion which, by its very nature, arouses suspicion, since to remember is, after all, only a more down-to-earth way of imagining), as though this motion, already suspect in its essence and which I cannot envisage without vertigo, turned out to be more disturbing when I try my skill at giving an account of old vertigoes and even more disturbing in the case of a story like this one which, centering upon a doubt about time, also contains the piquancy of being doubtful in itself.

"*Consommé*," [consommé] which is merely the more distinguished verbal envelope in which, in a restaurant, bouillon is served. "*Consommation*," [drink in a café] which for me designated, at first, certain metal tokens won in mechanical games in bistros and which one could exchange for a drink (I knew nothing about these penny machines and I was also unaware that *consommations* were things one drank, but occasionally I would receive a little coin like that from the pocket of one of my uncles, who had no doubt won it in the café but hadn't wanted to use it—the uncle I had hardly ever seen order anything else, if he had to have an apéritif, but innocent *madère-citrons* [Madeira-lemonades]). "*Tout est consommé*" [all is consumed] coming after the wine mixed with gall and the sponge soaked in vinegar, "*consommation des siècles*" [drink of the centuries] in bell bronze like the "*confusion des langues*" [confusion of tongues] and like the "*fruit de nos entrailles*" [fruit of our womb]: expressions learned at the time of my catechism and differentiated absolutely, by their too serious sound, from *consommé* and *consommation*, which are liquids that one drinks; expressions assuredly too heavy, one with the death-agony, the other with the end of the world, for me to be able, even now, to make this comparison without feeling I am yielding to a low cabaret wit by indulging in the most pernicious sort of play on words.

Yeux du bouillon [specks of fat on soup, lit. eyes of the bouillon]. *Yeux qu'on roule en boules de loto* [eyes that one rolls like lotto chips]. In contrast to these eyes in the plural are the eagle's eye, the sparrow-hawk's eye, the lynx's eye, the viper's eye. In sum, what you see are *eyes* but it is *an eye* that looks at you (or it is with that singular eye that you look). Inside, the two black chambers that we supposedly have in our heads (but it is only true viewing the thing this way from outside, because inside, we don't experience any of it) with those two skin-thin lenses; outside, the beyond-the-grave air assumed by what is diorama, scene artificially lit and inserted in space, as by everything that seems arranged so that we may recognize in it the external projection of the true chamber within—that well-sealed cavity which is the imaginary realization of what is called the "*for intérieur*" [conscience; lit., inner tribunal]—suddenly illuminated and changed to a sort of wax museum mortuary fixedness. Mortuary chapels, then, are many of the spectacles offered to the undivided gaze in which our two eyes spring into action—this being the case when these visions are marked, either by their very nature or by circumstances, by a certain theatrical air that half disengages us from life and when their content fulfills the supremely important condition of lending itself to our becoming, when confronted with them, King Claudiuses witnessing the reconstruction of our crimes, petitioners to whom a symbolic staging reveals the arcana of the initiation, prisoners condemned to death dreaming of our punishment as we see in certain pictures (with the guillotine or gallows in one of the upper corners in the middle of a little cloud), even a person whose eye—necessarily only one—is glued to a keyhole to spy on the unfolding of an erotic act in a closed room whose walls, floor, ceiling imitate the blinkers of his mind which is almost entirely obnubilated by the view of the salacious scene.

No doubt it is in the nature of underground caves, chasms, and everything that on the earth imitates, on a gigantic scale, the concavity of a mouth, to engender an apprehension that one will always have to overcome, even if this recovery of oneself takes place instantaneously and practically without effort. As is perhaps the case with the uneasiness experienced in darkness (that other sort of cavern in which we already feel swallowed up, quite apart from the many other dangers that threaten us), it is possible that such an apprehension must be associated with the childish fear we have of being eaten, the most rudimentary form of aggression among all those to which we may imagine our presence in the midst of the world exposes us, during that phase of mental life in which we are still so close to the state of the baby who scarcely emerges from his sleep except to suck on his mother's breast or ingest food in some other way. Isn't it possible that death, which Christian allegories represent as a skeleton with empty sockets and very conspicuous teeth, might be—with the two black holes that it uses as eyes, and its sadistic ogre's rictus—the dark, gazeless thing that will eat us some day? It is the memory of a veritable incursion into the bowels of death (as though I had been devoured quite raw by the monster just as the initiates of many ancient cults were supposed to have been), the memory of coming into contact with the abyss or of a descent into the underworld that I have preserved from certain touristic excursions or various other circumstances that led me to visit underground caves, quarries, or, at least, to find myself confronted with what passed, in my eyes, for such.

The famous well of Padirac (where I went just once, in 1934) has at first something comical about it, outfitted as it is with a building on the facade of which one reads: *"Entrée du Gouffre"* [entrance to the abyss] written in big letters as though this were an attraction like some *Train fantôme* [ghost train] or *Rivière mystérieuse* [mystery river]. Having passed through the entrance gate, one gets on an elevator and descends into a vast natural cylinder (or sort of upside down gasometer) which, just a few meters down, includes a ledge on which a *"Restaurant de la Terrasse"* [terrace restaurant] has been constructed; after the elevator, a number of stairways, and a gallery that one walks along, one arrives at a dock on the bank of the underground river. Up to that point, nothing really sensational: a geological curiosity such as one might imagine, arranged very much à la Jules Verne. The amazement will come with the excursion by boat on the wrinkle-less river: lofty vaults, of course, with stalactites and, at every moment, rocks of fantastic shapes whose names the boatman unfailingly gives you, all indicative of creatures or objects that they evoke; but—and this is the surprising thing—the vault is sometimes reflected in the water, in appearance completely motionless, so perfectly that one forgets the existence of that water and can believe that the skiff is moving without support over a plane strictly median to a double vault of which one does not know, in many spots, which appears the more vertiginous, its zenith, situated at a height to which it would seem that neither ceiling nor cupola of any human construction could attain or its nadir, which is the exact replica and toward which the same walls, inverted, lead. No outdoor spectacle, I think, could impress me to the same extent as did this immensity in an airtight chamber, where earth and sky were repudiated and where infinite space, engulfed at the bottom of an enormous pocket, appeared as a content and not as an envelope.

"Ici chambres à coucher pour géants" ["rooms to let for giants"] was the graffito I read three years later in one of the quarries of Les Baux-de-Provence, those extraordinarily elevated and spacious recesses, half-caves, half-architectures, which resemble Egyptian sanctuaries carved right into the rock and remind one of the cave in which, in the last act of *Aida*, the young officer of the pharaoh and the Ethiopian captive who became his lover were walled up, dying. In the quarry which some practical joker had imagined transformed into a caravansery for titans, a large skeleton equipped with a scythe had also been drawn and it was also at Les Baux that—one of the times we went there on foot from Saint Rémy, where we had settled for the duration of the

summer—my wife and I visited a *Grotte aux Fées* [fairy grotto], a quite
ordinary cave, in truth, but from which departs, so it is said, a subterranean gallery so long that it goes all the way to Arles, where it emerges
under the amphitheater. Isn't it the case that a place like the amphitheater of Arles—where Spanish-style and Provençal-style bullfights
are held nowadays—adds to its glory as monument a prestige current
enough for it to be one of the most important spots in a region? And
furthermore, should one be surprised that in this same region, where
quarries have been worked since the time of the Romans, the popular
imagination should have worked on the idea of an almost magical
communication between one of these ancient constructions of which
Arles, Nîmes, and their environs still bear the ruins and a spot like Les
Baux, so spectral with its old abandoned palaces, their gaping case-
ments scarcely distinguishable from the elements of some necropole
or dormitory for workers from Babel hollowed out of the rock by the
quarrymen? It is probably difficult to escape the summons of fable as
soon as there is a grotto, quarry, any sort of hole giving the impression
of a vestibule—if not a domanial parcel—of the subterranean world,
confused with the world of death in countries like ours where people
are buried.

In the immediate outskirts of Saint Rémy, not far from the place
called the *"Plateau des Antiques"* [Plateau of the Antiquities], there
are quarries; and we discovered it by chance, without knowing at the
time what we were seeing: old Roman mines abandoned today. Having
been determined, the very evening we arrived, to take a look at the
little triumphal arch and the mausoleum that constitute the "Antiq-
uities," we saw nearby the beginnings of a path and, wanting to prolong
our before-dinner walk a little, also curious to know where this path
led, we started off on it, even though by that time, at the end of the day,
and on such a path, bordered on both sides by shrubbery and under-
brush, it was already very dark. After a few bends and a brief descent, I
found myself all at once face to face with an immense screen of blackness: total darkness looming up all of a piece and perfectly impenetrable; in all probability the opening of a vast cave, but appearing in such a
sudden manner and so closed to one's gaze that it was much more like a
portal leading to nothingness. If I was frightened by it, the feeling was
much less like the fear caused by a wall, a precipice, or any other
obstacle that had abruptly revealed itself and forced us to stop in our
tracks with the sensation of avoiding a collision or a fall than it was as
though really I were a few yards away from the threshold one crosses

when—to use the hallowed expression—one passes *"de vie à trépas"*
[from life to death]. A fear less sharp than the fear that may be aroused
by the imminence of an actual danger; a fear that, nonetheless, was
perhaps the more profound, for its object occurred in a pure state, as it
were, removed from any atmosphere of violence and without there
being present, to obliterate in me the quite naked dread of death, the
idea of a specific possibility of catastrophe toward which my entire
being would strain, actually forgetting what would be the unavoidable
consequence of such a brutal accident. When—the very next day—I
saw the place again in the full light of day, I realized that in fact what
the path led to was not a cave. Not a cave, but a sort of hall, obviously
carved by human hands in the rocky wall from which it opened out,
and the first of a long series, of which I walked through the less dark
ones, somewhat disgusted by the large, reddish bats that fluttered
about in them. In one of these excavations, I found several two-wheeled
carts, their shafts resting on the ground, which had been stored there as
though part of an encampment abandoned for a longer or shorter time
by creatures belonging to one of those epochs independent of all chronology evoked by certain rustic implements related to thatched roofs
and flocks of sheep; so that I liked to believe that here—two steps away
from the Alpilles, that strange chain of miniature mountains, scarcely
higher than the Russian mountains in an amusement park and arranged, sometimes, like a public garden where simulacra of ascents
have been planned for the strollers—there had once been an old lair of
smugglers or brigands like the cave spoken of in *Mémoires d'un âne*
[The Golden Ass] in the chapter where one sees the astute Cadichon
alert the guards with his braying and thus bring about the capture of
the band of highwaymen who had kidnapped him and taken him to
their hovel. Once back in town, I learned that I had been walking in
ancient quarries long since abandoned. The idea came to me of exploring them in depth; but when I went to the town hall to obtain the
necessary authorization, the official I saw kept trying to dissuade me
from it: the passageways went very far in; to explore their labyrinth, I
would need to equip myself seriously where light was concerned because of the holes and shafts I would perhaps encounter; in short, it
would be a real expedition. I therefore gave up on it, in the end; but I
returned several times to those quarries, and each time with the same
emotion. It was no longer the anguish of my first visit at nightfall
facing the curtain of absolute black beyond which I would have been
blinded, it was a much more mixed feeling: that of a child who, playing

at certain games, confronts dangers he knows very well are merely semblances of real dangers; that of a child, too, who finds himself in church, not necessarily in front of a crèche with rocks of papier-maché but, at least, within that other world reduced to proportions still imposing but habitable and purged of all mystery too poisonous by the ABC of its emblems and its imagery; the emotion, too, that one may feel in the wings of a theater where ropes, frameworks of flats, practicable doors together with what one divines of the trapdoors and the below-stages give the impression of a voyage into the infernal regions or of a masonic trial one must undergo without flinching, braving the risk of getting lost, coming up against an unexpected obstacle, committing a blunder that would lead one to fall suddenly in the visual field of mirthful spectators or suffer an ignominious exclusion after the collapse or puncture of a stage set. Much more than when touring the ruins of Eleusis, for example, I was able to imagine—as I visited the old Roman quarries of Saint Rémy after having stumbled upon their shadows—that I had penetrated into the *cavern of mysteries* and had emerged from it quite alive.

EDOUARD GLISSANT

Michel Leiris: The *Repli* and the *Dépli**

Et toute ta vie tu descendras l'escalier.

—Aurora.

For Michel Leiris, meticulousness in observation certainly did not justify a fragmented vision of reality, but rather led to a coiling-up of details, verified one by one, whose spiral accumulation led one to see the totality. This detailing, guarantee of veracity if not of truth, corresponded to a characteristic of his own nature. Withdrawn into himself, prudent and suffering perhaps from timidity, he made an effort to take serious notice—neither fake nor indulgent—of others and of the world. Thus he read reality with a sort of deliberate *forcènement* [frenzy] or delight, precisely because he was wary of his own natural distraction or his egotism. He related what he read to what he knew of himself, looking for a correlation between the two. Thus, he always came back to Michel Leiris, but only out of modesty and out of fear of creating or imposing established or definitive truths.

For him, then, reality is only a totality on the condition that all conclusive claims are left out of this term. This totality is incessantly weaving its own plot.

Leiris's passion is to rummage through this plot, not just anywhere, but in every little corner where he might surprise himself, in every place where he might find himself implicated in the Other, and in every word that would put this relationship at stake. It is in one of his first books, *Aurora* ("I wasn't yet thirty when I wrote *Aurora*. . . "), a

---

*Because the English translation does not offer the same sense of the two terms, I have retained the French for *repli* and *dépli*. They could be translated as "withdrawal," as in the French expression *"replié sur soi-même,"* and "opening-up" or "unfolding" for *dépli*.—Translator's note.

YFS 81, *On Leiris*, ed. Blanchard, © 1992 by Yale University.

phantasmagoria of the Voyage, that Leiris describes such comings and goings, illustrated by this example:

> The death of the world equals the death of myself. No disciple of any wretched religion will ever make me deny this equation, the only truth which dares aspire to my approval, although on the contrary I sometimes sense all the vague chastisements and monstrous threats which the word HE could hold for me.[1]

Reality is a single body of meanderings, and life (Leiris's life) is the echo that bounces off the twists and turns of this meander. Reality and its corresponding life constitute *repli*. From their union (in the idea that Leiris has of it), a rhetoric is born: an art of telling that aims to illuminate rather than to convince, to persuade himself rather than to confuse the reader—the mute confidant—with an overabundance of explanations.

This is the very practice which governs the observation, or vision, in *L'Afrique fantôme*. If the title of this book sets up a presupposition (for it is Leiris himself who plays the phantom, looking for, but unable to find himself), the contents of the book do not drift off into theoretical suppositions. Although the field of ethnography should have imposed upon Leiris the most stringent objectivity in observation according to the practice of the time, in this work, he establishes rather a sustained relationship between subjectivity and reality, one which would be the foundation of his life's work.

Three distinct orientations thus constitute the organization of *L'Afrique fantôme:* subjectivity, which intrudes into ethnological thought; the relationship to the other, which implies modesty; and suspense, or the desire not to conclude with a generalizing theory.

We will venture to say that suspense is one of the major elements of the art of Michel Leiris's prose, a suspense which does not appear in "leaps and bounds," but which stretches out in duration—or in space—as does the act of writing and its flexibility.

At that time, a conception of "pure" ethnology prevailed in which one attempted to discover the dynamics of any given society, with the understanding that these societies were also "pure," or in any case less complex. However, the claims of this dominant ethnology were quite contrary to what we have seen in Leiris's work. They were founded on

1. Michel Leiris, *Aurora*, trans. Anna Warby (London: Atlas Press, 1990), 54. Hereafter cited in the text.

the basis of the following: objectivity, or the desire to discover the essentials of any given social or cultural phenomenon; distancing, by which one sought to guarantee this objectivity; and definition, or general conclusion (theory), by which one displayed a total understanding of the observed phenomenon—and by which one attempted to increase the power of understanding to include the analysis of other phenomena, supposedly of the same nature.

Leiris does not succumb to the temptation of the generalizing universal. It is not truth that he attempts to learn here, but first and foremost, his truth, limited and complex: his relationship to the other. This relationship is also a *repli*.

His most significant work in this regard is *Contacts de civilisations en Martinique et en Guadeloupe*, a book which is rarely talked about, and for good reason: how can one analyze this supercilious accumulation of facts and observations that lead to no underlying theories, but only brush up against reality, making do by interweaving it within this massive description? With the practical and humble manner that was his in the face of facts, things, and people, here the ethnographer Leiris consents to common paradigms of anthropology and sociology: the study of social classes, the meeting between levels of language, the examination of historical *"formations"* (constructs), etc. We are quick to acknowledge, however, that when confronted with the complex reality of the francophone Antilles, what interests Leiris is not the essence of this reality (to discover or "understand"), but primarily the complexity itself as essence. Here, we are right in the midst of an ethnology of *Relation*, of an ethnology of the relationship to the other. *Contacts* is one of Leiris's most "calm" books just as if he hadn't implicated himself in it. But this, indeed, is where he takes his greatest pleasure in accumulating, interweaving, and then suspending. In this he rediscovers his own complexity, which to him is the only one that is truly analyzable.

To study the contacts between cultures is already to decide that one has no lesson to learn form it, no conclusions to impose, for it is the nature of these contacts to be *fluente*, unexpected. We will conclude then (relating the quality of this observed reality, or the account of it, to the observer himself) that Leiris did not expect to bring any conclusions to his self-analysis, unless it was to envision day after day this other conclusion, that is also a suspense, and that obsessed, or rather, mesmerized him: the moment of his death. Not death as a possible horror (as Montaigne tried to deal with it in advance), but death as a mystery or a scandal, putting an end to another scandal and mystery, that of life: *"Nuit et jour la mort me surplombait comme une morne menace"*[2] [Day and night death hung over me like a mournful threat [90].]

However, if observation of reality and confession do not aspire to the discovery of the essence of things, what's their use? We know the answer concerning ethnography: it is a matter of describing with integrity in order to better establish the *Rapport*, to better form the basis of exchange. As for confession, wrapped up as we are in the interweavings of the work, we do not immediately perceive one of the obvious points. Leiris, in truth, does not furnish us with the elements of "his" life— women whom he loved, regrets he had, etc.—except in a secondary and somewhat illusory manner.

This is because confession for Leiris does not come at all close to what we understand as confession in Rousseau: the exaltation of the I, or even the justification of an existence or of a thought. No more, let us repeat, does it conform to the quest for an indubitable truth.

Nevertheless, it is the same unmerciful demand for veracity in detail that imposes itself here (in confession) and there (in the practice of ethnography). The scrutiny with which Leiris looks at the world is constrained within the permanence of this veracity, in which the confession is the most difficult vector to sustain. For Leiris, it is the eye which is most demanding. The eye which sees in the present, but also in memory, that *hears* words, expressions, ritornellos, sayings. As Claudel said: "The eye listens. . . ."

And so we discover the principle of confession in Leiris's work that we had predicted at first. It is truly a matter of creating a rhetoric which alone is capable of providing an excuse for the scandal that is, for him, the human condition, that is to say, his condition. *"Ce n'est pas impunément que l'on vient sur terre et toute espèce de fuite est impossible"*, (*Aurora*, 58) [We do not come into the world with impunity, and there is no possible escape [69].]

The demand for veracity is therefore unavoidable: if the elements of rhetoric set into place (words, expressions, ritornellos, sayings with which the author first sets out, or the events which he uses) were deformed, fantasized or fabricated, then the link between condition and expression would be broken. And if we confused the one for the other of these two dimensions (the human condition and the ex-

2. Michel Leiris, *Aurora* (Paris: Gallimard, 1977), 84. Hereafter cited in text.

pression which is assumed to come with it) we would return, purely and simply, to the essentials of this scandal of existence without having been able to avoid it. The artifice of art does not consist in forcibly relating the veracity of facts to the circle of subjectivity, but rather to unveil the relationship, if there is one, between the fact and oneself, and vice versa. It is with the phrase "if there is one" that the rhetoric begins and it is also there that it finds its justification. The art of writing, the only true "exploration," is a stage of the possible.

Michel Leiris is neither essentialist nor minimalist. He doesn't intend to define anything. He attempts to establish this relationship between the inconceivable system of existence and the resolute system of expression. This relationship is neither fusion nor confusion. The meticulous eye is therefore also a rhetorical eye. Confession is a discourse, an architecture of the spoken that tends to facilitate an exorcism.

From the elements that life has laid out, word games are constituted, or rather, the word game in which the combination *"en abyme"* procures rhetoric. We would sum up the process of the operation thus: discourse organizes what existence procures. To state it better, defining it as closely as possible: *ce que le repli a recélé, la rhétorique le déplie* [rhetoric uncovers what withdrawal has concealed].

From the *repli* to the *dépli,* movement is incessant.

In terms of these objectified elements of existence that are objects, we remark this notation which inscribes the coming and going of the *repli-dépli:* *"Une telle série d'objets, étagée comme un flux, doit nécessairement en voir une autre lui succéder comme étant le reflux,"* (*Aurora,* 62) [Such a series of objects, tiered like waves at high tide, must of necessity be followed by another representing, as it were, the low tide (72).]

We conceive of how here Leiris shares, but also rises above, the surrealists' passion for bric-à-brac, for the chance meeting of foreign objects, chosen by existence, and from which their lists proceed from Guillaume Apollinaire's "Il y a . . ." For Leiris, these lists are reversible, contaminating. *Repli-dépli.*

When we say "rhetoric," we do not mean by that a body of precepts knowingly put into place, nor a didactic ruse, but rather a daring dynamic of speech, a bet that exposes itself, and in which the field covers the conjunction outside-inside, oneself-world, existence-expression.

Leiris's prose is a metaprose with a level of expressibility (when he "confesses" the "facts") and a level of reflexibility (when he relates confession to the equivalence that we stated: from the *Haut mal* of life to the *Frêle bruit* of speech. However, the two levels cannot be separated: doing so would be to deny the project of enterprise itself. Like reality, prose is interwoven.

We can locate here complex procedures of contamination: semantics, for example, one of the first illustrations of which is proposed in *Aurora*—where the name of the heroine gives rise to all sorts of comparisons or of derivative signifieds (OR, AURA, OR AUX RATS, HORRORA, O'RORA)—and where Leiris writes this, which is a prelude to a number of *enchaînements* from *La Règle du jeu:*

> I reflected on what I had seen and, watching the pole star glinting softly like the ironic point of the two-edged sword of Paracelsus above the hangar now transformed into a charnel-house. I contemplated the name Aurora, inextricably linked to the destiny of this astonishing girl who was now being carried off by the last shreds of cloud towards a skyscraper constructed (from what immutable cement?) on the edge of a continent obscure yet extraordinarily light and enduring, and I remembered that in Latin the word *hora* means "hour," that the stem *or* is found in *os, oris* which means "mouth" or "orifice," that it was on Mount *Ararat* that the Ark came to rest after the Flood and finally, that if Gérard de Nerval hanged himself one night in a back street of central Paris, then it was because of two semi-spectral creatures each of whom bore half of this name: Aurélia and Pandora. [163]

Geographic contaminations, or collusions of places inferred from semantics and many other forms of tranversalities, are expressly related to procedures of alchemy, or of transmutation: from outside to inside, and inversely, from existence to speech, from life-death to rhetoric that alone can provide an excuse for it, for want of illumination.

Leiris's prose is one long gasp hacked up by deep or held breaths, as for someone who doesn't cease to see coming a fragile apocalypse, which he intends to assume.

What we would call in Leiris the poetic aspect of poetry, or let us say it, the writing of the poem, was a preliminary moment, the unveiling of *repli:* it is the tranquil passion for prose that organizes the revealing *dépli.*

Following this, meticulousness in observation is doubled by an equal meticulousness in the organization of the discourse. Rhetoric recomposes the pure residue of the stove where life is boiling.

I have cited *Aurora,* and only this book, in order to emphasize that the almost obsessive enterprise of Leiris was, from the beginning of his itinerary, in him and wholly his.

I am surprised to find there already, for example, the evocation of this state that, for him, was boredom, that was neither the blues nor melancholy, and that he confessed to feeling to visiting friends in the last moments of his life. Michel Leiris is bored when he is not pursuing this correlation that we have examined here (from the *repli* of existence to the *dépli* of writing). I do not conclude that he lived to write, but certainly that writing did not satisfy him if he could not find in it the grounds for living. Boredom is the vacuity that sometimes displays its gloomy indifference in the rejection of these two demands: the constraint of living and the pleasure of writing.

This is why Leiris's poetics could be conceived thus: to always insert the cadenced rigor of writing into the shapeless mass of lived experience. *Aurora* tells us that in its provocative and exacerbated manner:

> At this point I must tell you that for me life has always been synonomous with everything soft, lukewarm and undefined. Liking only the intangible, that which is no part of life, I arbitrarily identified all that is cold, hard or geometric with this constant, and it is for this reason that I love the angular lines which the eye casts into the sky to apprehend the constellations, the mysteriously premeditated order of a monument and finally the ground itself, the most perfect plane locus of all figures. [90]

Just as Reverdy tried to give us the ability to touch the roughness of things, even through a poem, Leiris wanted to unfold speech that would be a live fabric, patient and revealing, of those very things that are true to the one who lives them, feels them, and refuses to name them in an ideal conclusion. Reverdy seeks ineffable contact, and Leiris the *Relation* that states itself.

For, indeed, the last word of his rhetoric—according to and through the *report* of reality, and the signifying *déport* of writing—lies completely in the ambition of a real—liberated—relationship to the other.

—Translated by Cynthia Mesh

FRANCIS MARMANDE

Michel Leiris: The Letter to Louise

Poet, ethnologist, writer, Michel Leiris changed the rules of auto-biography (*L'Age d'homme, La Règle du jeu*), the rules of the relationship to others (*L'Afrique fantôme*), and the profound connection with language (*Langage tangage*).

The meaning of his loyal friendships (André Masson, Alfred Métraux, Georges Bataille, Kahnweiler, Georges Limbour, Sartre, Picasso, Bacon . . .) lies in his role as *mediator:* mediator between literature and facts, poetry and action, the arts and the social sciences.

From the Dakar-Djibouti expedition where Marcel Griaule took him along in 1931, Michel Leiris returned as an ethnologist (in his own way). His personal diary, *L'Afrique fantôme* (1934), an unexpected sequel to Raymond Roussel's *Impressions d'Afrique*, annoyed the professionals as a faux-pas. "*On ne peut jamais tout dire, c'est entendu, mais dans l'Afrique fantôme, je voulais dire le maximum*" [It's impossible to say everything, agreed, but in *l'Afrique fantôme* I wanted to say as much as possible]. The excess of subjectivity and sensitivity, that critical part of the groundwork, is surprising . . .

Upon his return, Marcel Griaule published his study on *Les Masques Dogons*. Meanwhile, Leiris engaged in a perfectly respectable presentation of *La Langue secrète des Dogons*. This is a serious piece of work, in the style of his other work on *La Possession et ses aspects théâtraux chez les Ethiopiens de Gondar* (published in 1958). His scientific critic, however, deplored the work's lack of rational organization, what he called its "explosions successives de pensées" [successive explosions of thought]. But Leiris did not take offense. Indeed, he was enchanted with the formula and went back to work for publication.

YFS 81, *On Leiris*, ed. Blanchard, © 1992 by Yale University.

Language, secrets, possessions, ritual comedy, identity, masks: in a sense, all that preoccupies Leiris is there. It is enough to listen to the words.

Through the names which fascinated him without his knowing it (*Godon, Gondar*), through these unused glossary words, whose letters seem to be distributed like a sign addressed by ageless peoples, Leiris's tension exerts itself only upon that which he chose to name. In an intimacy open to the world.

"JAZZ—JASE EN ZIGZAG. JE JOUE, JE JOUIS, JE GEINS!" [JAZZ—BABBLE IN ZIGZAG. I PLAY, I REACH ECTASY, I MOAN!]*

It is by way of jazz that Leiris came to ethnology. At the close of the war, beginning with the early twenties, the luminous outpouring of black voices and rhythms called out to him like a summons. Exoticism sent the civilization of modern cities writhing. The joyous, spectacular explosion of these *mélanges*, of these impossible encounters (the dream of Africa, plus the industrial development) overwhelmed him all the more because of its overtly erotic implications.

Chance (objective, of course) did the rest. At *Documents*, the journal founded by Georges-Henri Rivière and sustained by Georges Bataille, Leiris met Griaule. That was in 1929. He detached himself from surrealism to which he had adhered without reservation. He got on better with Aragon than with Breton. From 1922 forward he was closely united with André Masson and from 1924 forward with Bataille. It was friendship that counted most for him. Soon after Bataille—and this is a first in French letters—Leiris took his turn on the couch of Doctor Borel, who had himself been analyzed by Lowenstein, who had been seen by Freud. Psychoanalysis and ethnography led him back to literature. He thought he could sacrifice the vanity of literature when he was with the Dogon people or in Gondar. During this two-year journey he attempted to forget it. But literature recaptured him.

For this reason it has been claimed, a bit hastily, that in his autobiography Leiris thus made himself into his own ethnologist.

*Note the word-play on *jazz* and *jase*, and *joue, jouie, geins*—Translator's note.

The formula is nice, tempting. But it only registers an approximate awareness of the enterprise inaugurated by *L'Age d'homme* (1939) and pursued in *La Règle du jeu* (1/*Biffures*, 1948; 2/*Fourbis*, 1955; 3/*Fibrilles*, 1966; 4/*Frêle bruit*, 1976), and to which *Le Ruban au cou d'Olympia* (1981), *Langage tangage* (1985) and *A Cor et à cri* (1988) may be added as a codicil.

THE BRUTALITY OF FACT

How exactly can the (little) worries about his sexuality or the methodical curiosity about wordplay be linked with an ethnographic concern? For Picasso as for Leiris, the "brutality of fact" (the expression comes from Francis Bacon) was the essential requirement. In order to reach it, Leiris took words literally. He listened to what language was telling him; language, his first interlocutor, the only one to pose nakedly the question of poetry and the question of truth.

For the ethnographer as in confession (confession, secret, or avowal?), only the pursued objective is the same: to formulate a kind of general anthropology. To remain in a compromised equilibrium between extreme interiority and the most remote *ailleurs*, on that ridge where the subject breaks apart more than it holds together. To maintain right up to the very end the ambition of showing the hidden faces of the cards (which is only a beginning), but above all to redistribute them, so as to make writing and life coincide at last. "Je me suis aperçu un jour que ce livre relatif à ma vie était devenu ma vie même" [I realized one day that this book about my life had itself become my life]. Or at least to give it a try.

A picturesque detail: the writer works with the help of index cards just like an industrious ethnographer. . . . As you can see, we are a far cry from automatic writing (*l'écriture automatique*). Leiris's aim was not only to reach those associations of ideas at which he excelled, those disassociations of letters to which he devoted or abandoned himself, those wordplays he incited: what he wanted to find were *associations of facts*.

GLOSSAIRE, J'Y SERRE MES GLOSES
[GLOSSARY; TO PACK, TO CROWD]

This is not Leiris's only paradox. *Images de marque*, his most recent book, strings them together with a dryness at once cruel and voluptuous: "*Un crabe à la démarche oblique*" [A crab with a diagonal walk]; "*Un énergumène qui n'a jamais cassé de vitre*" [A roughneck who has never broken a window]; "*Un révolutionnaire que ses habitudes paralysent et que la vue du sang ferait presque blêmir*" [A revolutionary who is paralyzed by his habits and who would almost go white at the sight of blood]; "*Un athée adorateur de la lune*" [An atheist who worships the moon]; "*Un positiviste qui a faim de miracles*" [a positivist who hungers for miracles], etc. Such paradoxes make us laugh, tremble. They seem too literally lapidary. Formulas or inscriptions, last words engraved in passing, they alone in their ultimate lightness make it possible to fathom paradox, contradiction, as a tension, a difference in potential, a break.

Well brought up, Leiris did not fear insolence. Rather reserved, he consented to excess. Rather cautious, he did not hesitate to take radical positions at the necessary moment (anticolonialism, antiracism, antifascism). Extremely private, he appeared as one of the most exposed writers of the century. Dreaming of unlimited elsewheres, he took root. Eager for self-effacement, he saw his name offered up by his companion, Louise, to one of the most important galleries of contemporary art: the Louise-Leiris Gallery. (In 1939, to thwart the threats of the Nazi occupation, Louise took over the work of Kahnweiler.) A timid little man effaced by his own self-portraits, he was to have his portrait painted by the greatest artists of the century (Masson, Picasso, Bacon, Giacometti . . .).

In what he regarded as his "*devoir de lucidité*" (duty of lucidity), that work of ultimate denudation, which secured him a unique as well as essential position in the century, he knew that there was no recourse other than this threatened equilibrium between the internal and the external, between the abyss of the self and the desert of objectivity— somewhat like Henri Michaux in *Ecuador* or René Char in *Les Feuillets d'Hypnos*. It was only at this price, on this untenable condition, that he could succeed in saying the little he knew, yet *everything* he knew, about what it meant to be a man during that era. To remain standing, eyes wide open despite the awareness of lack and the distress seeping from it. . . . And to continue right up to the very end to string together sentences which more or less keep their balance, as a simple and verifiable manifestation of this enduring continuity.

The subjectivity under which narcissism crumbles (even if that subjectivity is not devoid of coquetterie) at least makes it possible to consider the appreciable margin of "calculated error," which has as its horizon—in Bataille as well, though it is less noticeable—the infinite dream of poetry.

"MAMMIFÈRE—MA MÈRE L'ÉTAIT, IL FAUT M'Y FAIRE . . . "

Autobiography? If you wish: it's been said so many times, in any case, that we'd better get used to it. . . . However, the "I" that writes itself could very well be, a bit ironically, the very "I" of lyric poetry which the dream of science brings back to the stage.

This is perhaps what explains the fact that we cannot deduce a single sustaining biographical thread in Leiris's "autobiography" with its reinvented rules. It conceals as much as it reveals.

Rimbaud set autobiography on the course of this hallucinated realism. But Rimbaud had to let go of everything. Mallarmé, on the contrary, whose every adventure signaled that he was never a dupe, that he knew what it was all about, guided the secret language of this hunter of Dogon secrets. Sent off by a preface ("De la littérature considérée comme une tauromachie": one of the most beautiful of the genre) which conceals his fears under a layer of light and undecidable humor, we will guard ourselves against seeing in the autobiographical act nothing but its share of risk (which is certainly there!) and in the pen a final, fatal thrust *de muerte*. Let us remember that we owe to Leiris, repentant *aficionado*, the most incisive pages on the roles of sacrifice and play, pages in which the dark comedy of the *corrida* [bullfight] is reflected (*Miroir de la tauromachie*, 1937).

The true risk of writing lies elsewhere. More muted, more moving, more shadowy, it is none other than the unavowable risk that literature, in essence—always that inherited suspicion of Dada!—is no more than a comedy about the danger of being. Flatter, more decisive, it is no more than the risk of facing our own stupidity. And, in passing, of hitting the bottom of rather vain contradictions.

Distrusting sentences, but delighting in loops, curls, in the circular movement of periodic sentences, in the baroque play of writing. . . . Distrusting literature, but drawing from it life's only color, its only calm. And all things considered, when one has been the man given to impossible oscillations, to the difficulty of being, to the will to die, to self-deception, to the in-between, having no other dream, no other toy than that sovereign talent where hesitation is suspended, for lack of resolution, between sound and sense, that arbitrary crack which is no less unbearable than that precarious existence in the world . . . "qui n'est pas moins insupportable que la pauvre présence au monde". Leiris's glosses open themselves up to infinity like the cry of a child aimed at that body which the mother tongue conjures up. ("*Mammifère, ma mère l'était, il faut m'y faire*").

To this impulse which the painful refusal of fecundity (remaining an "être-pour-rien," as Barthes would say) and the obsessive fear of suicide underline, there was only an imperfect yet irreplaceable recourse, a type of drug whose users are "les autres" as well: writing, this very real illusion of escaping from the clutches of death.

It is this chemistry of meaning, this alchemy of dream, that led Leiris to *se noircir* [blacken himself]. When it comes to writing, he is to himself his own "*nègre*" [ghostwriter].* He casts upon himself the same gaze he does on the "Nègres" of Africa or the Antilles (regarding a close friend of Aimé Césaire, we use "nègre" as Michel Butor does: on purpose. The dream never has a hidden meaning. It is already a story: a story taken for life and life for a dream. The temptation to blacken himself, thus, was what Leiris sought in the illusory lucidity of intoxication.

His unparalleled approach established a distance that had seemed unattainable. It invented a new objectivity that cruelly said "I". This approach is indebted to Montaigne and Nerval as much as to Proust and Roussel. Larousse, Littré and Grevisse provided him with indispensable resources, given his interest in language. Leiris never invented anything. He crossed things out. And if he crossed out, it was in order to achieve the exactitude of fact.

Crossing out on the page, he was never to cease linking together the irreconcilable in life (Surrealism, the Collège de Sociologie charged with the study of the sacred, existentialism), the fields of knowledge in the process of definition (anthropology, linguistics, psychoanalysis), separate beings (Masson, Limbour, Bataille, Sartre, Picasso) with an inimitable sense of proximity and discreet flamboyance. He never failed to address himself to Louise, his very first *destinataire* [addressee], whose recent death had divided her from a work which could thereafter be regarded a "une longue lettre à cette coutumière et tendre confidente, sa compagne au clair regard" [a long letter to this customary and tender confidente, his companion with the limpid gaze].

---

*The primary meaning of the French word, "nègre," is "Negro" or "nigger." The English word, "ghostwriter," misses the double-entendre of the French, which represents ghostwriting as slave labor.—Translator's note.

From Dakar to Djibouti, Leiris kept a journal every night, sending her installments without even discovering that underneath the names which obsessed him (Dogon, Gondar), it was actually her name he had been rewriting all along: the name of Louise Godon.

—Translated by Abigail S. Rischin

JEAN-CHRISTOPHE BAILLY

A River with no Novel

The *Règle du jeu*[1] [*Rule of the Game*] is not a part or even the central part of Leiris's work, but rather the hearth, and this so ardently that the smallest fragment, even when apparently played by a different rule or rather on another terrain, eventually returns to find itself in accordance with the rules of the autobiographical game. The slow and commanding strength of this game's elucidation contaminates the entire work. In Leiris's case, autobiography doesn't come down to a question of genre or of essential characteristics; it is implicated in the literary act itself and in its resolution. *L'Age d'homme* [*Manhood*][2] appears as a prefiguration of this identification; for this reason, its celebrated preface, *De la littérature considérée comme une tauromachie*, can be considered a preface to Leiris's entire work, while at the same time serving as a kind of manifesto whose application extends beyond its own boundaries. The shadow of the bull's horn doesn't define itself simply as a personal epigraph, but also, in a humble act free of all ostentation, as a warning to anyone considering getting involved with literature, which is, as is well-known, the privileged space of vanity. The shadow of this horn, together with the toreador, chosen as a model because he risks his life for his art, indicates to the reader as well as to the author that memories are not what is at stake here; not memories, but the movement which loses them, hunts them down and uses them in an attempt to create an

1. Michel Leiris, *La Règle du jeu* (Paris: Gallimard, 1948–76), 4 vols.
2. ———, *L'Age d'homme* précédé de la littérature considérée comme une tauromachie (Paris: Gallimard, 1946); *Manhood*, trans. Richard Howard (New York: Grossman Publishers, 1963).

YFS 81, *On Leiris,* ed. Blanchard, © 1992 by Yale University.

undivided unity of experience and language—thus what is at stake in literature is autobiography.

Literature engaged by this assimilation to something other than itself, bullfighting is immediately declared active within and inseparable from the separation of the self from the other. Leiris's entire work follows this dissociation incessantly, allowing the subsequent entry of an almost intimidating sense of doubt. Between the subject-who-remembers and the one-who-is-remembered, neither chronology—which would correspond to a perfect distribution of roles—nor transparence can find a place. The speaking subject, whose voice is heard by the reader, is unable to organize the successive episodes according to a linear logic: there is no ribbon of retrospection unfurling from the past to the present. The weight of the past appears not as an inverted estuary, but rather as a faraway land which sends back distended echos. Aside from the writing which strings them together, these echos are brought together by a certain quality; Leiris designates this quality as "La tendance naturelle de [sa] mémoire à retenir dans la somme prodigieuse de choses qui, de même qu'à tout homme, [lui] sont arrivées, celles seulement qui revêtent une forme telle qu'elles puissent servir de base à une mythologie" (*Fourbis*, 21–22)[3] [The natural tendency of (his) memory to retain, within the prodigious accumulation of experiences which he shares with all others, only those experiences whose form indicates the potential to found a mythology.] This "mythology," which this work attempts subsequently to establish, is in fact the interior criterion of memory. It is not so much a question of telling one's life as of proceeding from echo to echo in order to discern how this life has been woven together. In this way, the logical narrative structure of the *imparfait* conceals within itself a counterpoint indicated by the *futur antérieur;* within the mass of what happened is the call of what could have happened. Behind the figure of the writer are heroic figures who, following the example of the toreador, and despite the fact that they are borrowed from the innocent world of a child's imagination, become metaphors for the figure of the writer. These figures, of course, had to be abandoned; this is true of the jockey who rides through the pages of *Fibrilles*,[4] for example, a hero who triumphs in the face of adversity and independently leads his horse to victory against all odds. For if this extensively described figure is a memory of

3. ———, *Fourbis* (Paris: Gallimard, 1948–76).
4. ———, *Fibrilles* (Paris: Gallimard, 1948–76).

identification, it also becomes a kind of repressed other whose return forces literature to resemble itself.

Among all of the figures presented as so many examples of an abandoned virtuality at the heart of Leiris's work, however, there remains one which manages to incarnate itself and which in fact doubles Leiris's life: the ethnographer. It is nonetheless remarkable to observe how Leiris, beginning with the publication of *L'Afrique fantôme*,[5] blurs the clarity of this dissociation by constructing, with the very tools of an inquiry, an autobiographical work. It is even more remarkable to see how much this figure suffers from being put into action; as a dream, it was the starting point for a legendary or envious evocation, but when rendered real, this figure can only give realism. This deceptive virtue of reality is complex, and constitutes the core around which Leiris's work is organized. Reality, insofar as it is the first and last authority, appears simultaneously as the moment of the fall and as the moment of beginning or beginning again; the bull's horn is also reality, which is truthful and supports that which, living, is on the edge of death. While this authority destroys illusion, it functions at the same time as the reservoir where illusion can be revitalized. This is proof that getting carried away with oneself is forbidden, but also that it is possible to get carried away. Proof that one is only oneself, but proof as well that "oneself" is nothing more than a theater of consumed phantoms; proof that language, led astray by the real, must distinguish itself by seizing this real, but also proof that the real follows its own path, like a sublime and indifferent musical parade float. Because if the ethnographer is not the childhood jockey nor the writer the toreador, there exists nonetheless between these pairs a dance of exchanges which gives the last word alternately to the real or to language. Leiris's entire work can be described as the desire for the moment of seizure which would make the person at the center of these transactions solid and palpable; it could furthermore be described as the parallel interrogation which seeks to figure meaning as an absolute productivity made possible by a state of equilibrium between the different declensions of the source towards its echos. In the same way that language reels between the possibility and the impossibility of part of itself being a shadow of reality, the subject oscillates between what condenses him and what disperses him.

If it seems clear to the reader that this "person" becomes confused

5. ———, *L'Afrique fantôme* (Paris: Gallimard, 1951 [1934]).

with the writing subject whose name is Michel Leiris, it is equally clear that for this subject the whole business isn't so simple; for this subject, oscillating and lost, the real rule of the game is that the game cannot be finished, that the "subject" is not finite. It would be interesting to compare Leiris's attempt to Pessoa's—while the experience of transactions, for the Portuguese writer, is ordered according to the intervention of heteronyms and is played out within their vertigo, for Leiris this experience takes the form of an absolute homonymy. The autobiographical rigor, thus deprived of any possibility of escape on an imaginary level, resorts to feeling out, so to speak, the abyss of the subject. As a genre, however, autobiography remains faithful to a notion of the position of the subject which is both ancient and calm: that of a writer imagining his own past. And because it doesn't resemble a genre, autobiography, which is for Leiris movement itself, the very possibility of writing, can only be destabilized by such a position. The actual experience of the past is not equivalent to a retrospective representation, the subject who invokes this experience has come unglued, he is undone. The past presents itself in the form of what has gone away and what has returned, and the subject-who-remembers isn't the organizer of an accumulation of which he is king, but a wanderer, who leaves with what returns. What is sought after here by way of completion is only supported by the unsteady mass of memory, whose traversal is obligatory; this mass, though, by its very existence obstructs the purely active seizure which is dreamed of. This paradoxical and insoluble sequence can only result in the continuation of the work, its non-completion. An autobiography can never have the last word, this is left to death, which, with the authority of finality, subtends every word. An autobiography which constitutes itself as the experience of the abyss of the subject leaves itself no options, for it cannot finish with a final posture or restoration. The impossibility of this kind of academic restoration (a subject who lands on his feet like a gymnast after a dangerous manoeuver) is indicated by the very form of the continuation of the *Règle du jeu*: with *Frêle bruit*,[6] presented as the fourth and last volume, as with the books which came afterwards, it is the very density of the project which is undone, dispersing itself in shorter and shorter chapters, like an unfinished landscape. The destruction of the density and the impossibility of a restoration must not, however, be considered as failures but rather as the consequence of the project

6. ———, *Frêle bruit* (Paris: Gallimard, 1948–76).

undertaken. The impossibility of closure and of elucidation is the true nature of the "dreamscape of an enormous breadth" formed by the pages of the *Règle du jeu*, according to the definition given by the author himself. This immense detour away from fragmentation nonetheless ends with a fragment. The enigma of an existence is not resolved, but is instead unfolded before us, in a movement which incorporates the exegesis of the very progression of writing. The breadth of this unfolding, the discovery of an infinite number of folds hidden by other folds, and the *mise-en-abîme* of the seizure by its very project are what distinguish Leiris's story from all others. Paradoxically, digression is no longer a possibility in a narrative completely dominated by digression. In the boat headed for death, a sailor, in the mess, remembers the wake.

However, in this unfolding which precludes all possibility of completion as it grows vaster and vaster, this completion asserts itself, with a sporadic, uneven rhythm; it is acting within its rights, as if proving itself. This is not a question of happy moments which recuperate what has been lost: the *Règle du jeu* privileges these moments, but never gives them normative status or turns the game over to them. These moments both contain and communicate the possibility of an appeasement, an understanding: a precision of the relations between the subject-who-remembers and he-who-is-remembered, a resonance between the moment and the person gathering it so long after having experienced it. This form, which takes the theoretical expression of experience invested with the sacred, delineates a space characterized by a weightlessness between the I and the other of the story, as between the real and the imaginary. Leiris doesn't hesitate to qualify this unusual and momentary stabilization of the conflict inherent to the autobiographical project as poetry. What is at stake here is not a magic realism, or a magic becoming real, or the real raising itself up to the level of magic, but rather the sudden appearance of an imminent possibility, flashes, the precipitous surfacing of a mythical structure, points of condensation. The point of origin of these disruptions of equilibrium can only be considered as the product of an extraordinarily tense complexity: the last addition at the top of a house of cards which, contrary to all expectations, fails to collapse it. The work contains within itself all the crossed wires, all the connections, all the regrets necessary to maintain, if only for one instant, the image of access and of seizure; it accomplishes this by endlessly displaying the tactile matter, and we circulate across this matter as if it were a vast enumeration of causes whose ultimate effect is almost always delayed; the poem that is Leiris's prose is constituted by the eulogy of a purely evocative poem inserted in nuggets of time and language and given up as lost. But since the conditions of the appearance of this poem are inscribed in the very territory where it was lost, the text can only traverse this territory infinitely, like an investigation ricochetting from clue to clue.

The clue, as we know, is both the touchstone and the drive behind detective novels. Carlo Ginzburg has shown that the clue, which is the *régime* of the sudden appearance of signs, serves two functions: on the one hand, it extends far beyond the realm of detective fiction, while on the other hand, it appears as the modern avatar of the archaic *régime* of the trace.[7] The clue is that which, from the midst of an undifferentiated mass, distinguishes itself and makes a sign, not as an element of language, but as a signal in its pure form, a pure signature of difference. As such, it is isolated, but if it produces difference by means of an irruption, it immediately reabsorbs this difference in a chain reaction where it repeats itself; the clue produces a clue, difference produces meaning, which in turn is resemblance. In the detective story (or in psychoanalysis, where it takes the specific form of the symptom), this chain reaction is dependent on a certain narrative yield. In the case of the autobiographical inquiry, however, where the goal is not to resolve a crime or a completed intricacy but the entire enigma of existence, the distribution of clues is free of all narrative constraint, and spreads itself out in an infinite network, as resistant to completion as the inquiry which frames it and allows it to take shape. When Leiris speaks of "mythology," of the mythology which cannot be found, he means the structure of this network, which is at work behind its manifestations. This mythology isn't simply "structured like a language," but structured like the language through which it is unveiled, by which it is engulfed.

Biffures, Fourbis, Fibrilles, Frêle bruit—things crossed out, a disordered space, small fibers, small, fragile sounds—the landscape of meaning, hidden away in the minute, is in this way suspended in an immanence of interlacings and entanglements. The clue lives in a forest in which every tree hides the forest, where everything means something. The rule of the game, from this point on, forbids cheating with this contaminating virtue; it consists in allowing the forest to be

---

7. Carlo Ginzburg, translated from the Italian by Monique Aymard et al., *Mythes, emblèmes, traces* (Paris: Flammarion, 1989), 139–80.

seen through the chance of its rustling and the infinite harmony of its differences, without, however, going by way of the well-traveled paths, all of which are inscribed with an organization of meaning exterior to the forest's sudden appearance. Such a rule, for this very reason, excludes the novel; Leiris's project is *in no way* novelistic. As prose, this enterprise circulates in a network of poetry, and extends the "language of poetry" to the entire language. The clue holds within itself the difference of meaning; this difference contains the tonality of a contact each time specific: the memory of the thing is included in the word, a memory that makes the world resonate in the source of connections which constitutes the word.

But if Leiris's work is first and foremost prose work, it isn't like a diluted poem; that is to say, in accordance with the dilution of resonance in the disjointed textures of language and memory. In this way, the prosaic praise of poetry is transformed into a critique of poetic heroism, in which Leiris, although much more a "man of words" than Bataille, nonetheless shows his similarity to him. Leiris wants, as a poet, to reinvest language with the original violence which joins it to the occurence of meaning; he fails, however, to make an oracle out of this oracular virtue which he recognizes, or rather he subjects the oracle to the experience of prose. This is his realism.

The movement, however, which reveals the oracle in the digression and which wants simultaneously to provide the clue and its background, the resonance and the field of resonance, poetry, therefore, and prose, appears to be literally impossible. The person who refuses any rearticulation of the subject made available to him by the organization of meaning into genres or into sequences, the person who refuses the hymn, the novel, and the essay, finally comes up against the inability of language to be the entire language, and becomes suspicious of his very profession. Beyond his other dreams, beyond his lost jockeys, Leiris is an absolute writer, in exactly the same sense as people speak of a "literary absolute" referring to the incorporating theory of German romanticism. And it is as such, confronted with the pure limit of language, that he exorbitantly invests literature with the total identification with language, or in other words, not to be more limited than he himself is. In order to bring about such a project, the writer must enact the suicide of all his other selves (the novelist, the poet, the ethnographer and even the autobiographer) and replace them with figures (the toreador, the jockey), on whose shoulders falls the task of conveying what speaking (writing) means.

However, the desire to *be* literature, and in this abandon, to make literature coincide with that which in language is most original and most truthful, can only end up by encountering this double screen where literature falls short of the totality of language and where language in turn falls short of the totality of experience. Even if such a screen is to be considered despite everything traversable, even if every indication spotlights the potentiality of this passage, the long unfinished sentence inevitably comes back to live with the exegesis of its own failure. The ricochets are also consequences, the air and the water resist the thrown stone and the oracle is dissipated with a spatter of mud. It is Lichtenberg, not Leiris, who says "I would like the whip of a dazzled destiny to throw me across the world"; with, "I would have liked," however, this statement could function as the epigraph to Leiris's entire work.[8] The counterpoint of this epigraph is "Let words live," an expression which, in the meditation called *Langage tangage*,[9] constitutes the return of the bull's horn. As a wish, this expression admits doubt and permits the trembling of the unaccomplished. The way a voice animates vocabulary and grammar will never be *alive* enough to give language access to the absolute vitality where it would be equivalent to silence; why not, then, redefine the goal as pure and gratuitous sonorous adversity? If all of realism fails, why not let the cord vibrate for its own sake, as a purely bold resonance?

In the space where language had been put as close as possible to experience, where the will to capture was strongest, something suddenly comes loose; this space contains a truly ironic counterpoint, the part of Leiris's work where language, formerly relegated to being the being of resemblance, plays out its own logic, of its own accord, in the fracas of word games and deconstructed collections of sounds. This part of his work is always there, from *Glossaire* in 1939[10] to *Ce que les mots me disent* to *Langage tangage* (an essay on language which is in danger of being pulverized by word games); it functions as a secret supply and a provision for future needs which the consequential usage of words was unable to satisfy. The life of words becomes autocratic in word games, and becomes untranslatable in this movement of withdrawal. The untranslatable play of language is a wrench thrown into

    8. Georg Christoph Lichtenberg, translated from German and Preface by Martha Robert Denoël, *Aphorismes* (Paris: 1985), 200.
    9. Michel Leiris, *Langage tangage ou ce que les mots me disent* (Paris: Gallimard, 1985).
    10. ———, *Glossaire* (Paris: Gallimard, 1969).

the mechanics of meaning. A child who had initially sought to seize the body of language takes it apart and amuses himself with the pieces. This child, however, was the one who perceived words pronounced around him (*habillé en cour . . . le Point du jour . . . reusement*) completely differently from the adults who uttered them. It is in this way that the repeated return to word games doesn't simply reveal a childhood of language, but also a reverse (in the double sense of underside and failure, retreat) of adult language. The *Règle du jeu* thus becomes a huge detour taken by an experience in order to identify the lesson that that childhood error understood from the beginning. This lesson deprives language of all realist intent, and pushes it completely into the flow of legend.

This reunion with the flow of legend doesn't at all amount to an acquired or rediscovered "wisdom." On the one hand, this flow is like an underground river, whose resurgences guide the observable text by replenishing it. On the other hand, it's a detour through the observable text, which, like the main river valley, gives consistency to the secrets hidden beyond the resurgences. Leiris's work consists of poetry entering the space of prose, and transports the rustle of legendary matter into the texture of a life without legend, entirely related through stories. The structure of the "sacred in everyday life," as it was called during the era of the College of Sociology, is transformed, in literature, into a fabric which attaches the colored fibers of clues to the monochromatic background recitative. This fabric ends up being, in essence, woven—instead of harshly separating the designs from the background, it lets them enter gradually, as if it were a question of contamination. In passing from this textile metaphor to the operatic reference, we may observe that while Leiris's work also alternates between arias and recitatives, it attempts to unite them in an endless continuation; in this way, there is a mutual interference without opposition. One of the most common leitmotifs in the work, it is well-known, is the power of the human voice, the power of singing. Writing considers voice its superior, and makes the song, the *bel canto's* vertiginous feat, into a stasis which increases the rate of sensory liberation. But while writing privileges this song as if it were the same as the rustle of Lichtenberg's "dazzled destiny," it also knows that this song is contained, or rather detained, within writing itself, reserved like an impossible possibility, like its most intimate tension. Leiris consequently defines language "telle (qu'il) la conçoit, du moins à son altitude et vitesse de croisière": "pas plus linéaire et sèche que secouée de soubresauts mais chargée d'harmoniques et comme animée d'un indéfinissable *vibrato*. . . ." (*Langage tangage*, 94) [as (he) considers it, at least at its cruising altitude and cruising speed: its dry linearity is disrupted by jolts, charged with harmonics and animated by an indefinable vibrato.]

This vibrato is the "woven" fabric that I am talking about; it is the permanent intertwining of the design and the background, as well as the entirely fluvial desire for a reunited and harmonious literature, which would be able to carry off in its current all the reflections and decisions of meaning. This "river" carries away with itself the dream of an absolute performance and a complete resolution; it is like the desire for one sentence forever renewed, an entire and definitive book inviting language, from the beginning to the end, to be the unfurling yet calm violence of a continually informed strength. It was inevitable that at the heart of such an attempt, doubt about the working material would take a strategic position and function as a task. Word games and the decomposition of the words of language, despite their irony, are the residue of this task, and they act as a détente at the heart of the critical tension. These games are similar to scales that help the performer master his vocal or instrumental technique; in addition, beyond the fact that they decompose when played, they also insure a certain hygiene or maintenance of language. *Désir* (*desire*) becomes "*désert irisé*" [*iridescent desert*], *Jésus Christ* becomes "*gésier creux*" [hollow gizzard], or even life, which a "*Dé sépare du viDe*" [die separates from emptiness], (examples taken from the *Glossaire* of 1939). These are certainly pure word games, seemingly without consequence, but what is at stake here is still the vitalizing or revitalizing of words, whose meaning is always in danger of erosion through usage. The language which man ingenuously has at his disposal is similar to both the cinema of the Lumière brothers and that of Méliès. It is the echo of an event and conforms to a documentary rigor, even at the price of eliminating poetry through this erasure; however, it also divests itself of any reality and proclaims by its very being the right of fiction. Leiris's work exposes itself to a number of paradoxes surrounding the internal conflicts of language without shying away from them: the act of naming is both a pure act of reverence towards reality and a side step which distances it from reality whether the name given to a thing contains something of the ember and something of fireworks; a Baudelairian realism and an exacting desire for seizure coexist with the possibility of Raymond Roussel's work more than that of any other realist. "Let words live" could therefore be restated as "Let language be!" And let every name be the proper one: this would be the "dazzled destiny" of language traversed by the voice.

—Translated by Benjamin Elwood

JEAN-LUC NANCY

Les Iris

pour Irizarry, Manhattan.

(ne faites pas la liaison, ne faites pas le rapport non plus : ni la liaison des sonorités, telle que la langue française l'exige ici, ni le rapport des sujets, tel que la pensée, française ou pas, l'exige partout. Mais ne prenez pas non plus ce double interdit pour une introduction. Ni d'un côté, ni de l'autre, ne cherchez la clef, même s'il est clair que "les iris" est un pluriel de "l'iris", où l'apostrophe élide un "e" pour éviter un hiatus. Sans ce dernier, nous aurions ici "le iris", à quoi ne manquerait plus que la majuscule du nom propre pour être enfin l'auteur au programme d'aujourd'hui: "Leiris".)

Dites-vous plutôt que c'est parti : voilà, il fallait commencer, et c'est ainsi que cela s'est fait. On ne sait pas pourquoi, ou bien, il serait ennuyeux de le savoir. Ce qui précède est déjà ennuyeux à bâiller. C'est qu'un *hiatus* n'est pas autre chose qu'un "bâillement" : la bouche béante dans la vocalisation des voyelles amassées. La langue ne veut pas bâiller. La langue est sans cesse occupée, affairée, empressée, inquiète ou réjouie: elle ne lâche pas celui qu'elle tient. Leiris est tenu par la langue, jour après jour et pas à pas, infimement, intimement, minutieusement et précieusement tenu.

A pareille tenue, il n'y a pas d'accès. Nul ne touche à la langue de l'autre. Les idiomes ne se rencontrent jamais. Ils sont des parallèles, des parataxes, des particules dures. Chacun procède, dans son idiotie,

YFS 81, *On Leiris*, ed. Blanchard, © 1992 by Yale University.

d'une pression minime et irratrapable exercée sur la langue par une élocution. Chacun surgit d'une impression produite sur la langue et par la langue, une impression inimitable dans l'immense travail d'imitation de la langue. Fugace autant que durable, vague autant que précise. On part, on parle sous cette impression, jusqu'à l'âge d'homme et au-delà. On est déjà parti, et ce qui peut s'en suivre, on verra bien.

"On verra bien" : l'iris entoure la pupille. C'est par là qu'on voit, à ce qu'on dit. On voit par le trou dans lequel se laisse voir une petite poupée (soi-même, vous-même penché sur un oeil), et ce trou, cet opercule est entouré d'une iridescence, miroitement ou moirure d'arc-en-ciel, déesse pour tout dire, déesse du partage et de l'intimité des teintes. Arc teinté de la paix, d'une inaccessible paix autour de l'agitation des poupées. Déesse enserrant la poupée, moirures encerclant l'image.

(Iris est la messagère des dieux. Mais il s'agit ici de ce qui se passe lorsque les dieux n'ont plus de message à faire passer. Rien de violent, rien de spectaculaire, pas de "mort des dieux". Plus légère, plus sournoise aussi peut-être, une simple allée-et-venue quotidienne de signes, pulvérisée d'insignifiance—et pourtant, c'est comme une palabre jamais achevée avec un petit sphinx têtu. Il ne fait pas d'histoires, mais enfin, il s'obstine à marchander des énigmes de quatre sous. Il n'est pas question de jouer Oedipe. Il n'est pas question de se crever les yeux. Mais enfin, "l'homme" reste une devinette, jusqu'à son âge et au-delà. C'est comme une vieille habitude, dont on ne peut pas se défaire. Les Iris volètent un peu partout, porteuses de pas-de-messages, maix au sol il y a encore ce petit sphinx têtu.)

On verra bien—c'est-à-dire qu'il est possible qu'on ne voie rien, ou qu'il n'y ait rien à voir (comment distinguer ?).

Mais c'est ainsi que c'est parti, et que ça part toujours. Comme lorsque deux regards s'effleurent. Lorsqu'une moirure miroite un instant. L'instant est toujours trop bref pour être saisi. Ou plutôt : il n'est là que pour rendre sensible ce qui ne peut pas être saisi, ce qui n'est pas à saisir : une impression. La vocation de l'instant, ce pour quoi on l'appelle—"ô temps, suspend ton vol!"—, c'est le dessaisissement.

Celui-ci se démontre parfaitement identique au saisissement. Ce qui m'a saisi, m'a dessaisi de soi. Ce qui m'a saisi s'est dessaisi de moi, me laissant plus seul qu'il est pensable d'être seul. Seul à ne savoir de "soi" que le soubresaut solaire d'un miroitement qui ne s'est même pas illuminé, même pas éclairé. Iris pris sur le vide, pris sur le fait d'envelopper une pupille qui bée (hiatus) sur rien, sur la solitude de son "sujet". Car lui ne s'y voit jamais, comme on sait bien. Lui ne voit pas sa vision. Le sphinx a les yeux pleins de sable, d'éclats de mica et de vielles poussières d'os.

Pupille emmaillotée d'iris : minuscule momie d'Egypte au coeur de l'oeil. Bandelettes diaprées et serrées sur ce secret de rien : voir.

Il faut aller y voir soi-même. Cela se nomme "autopsie", *opsis* de l'*auto*, voir par soi-même, voir de ses propres yeux, ce qui s'appelle voir. Autopsie continue de l'existence ténue, anatomie de détails menus. Toutes ces choses qui nous saisissent, qui nous désaisissent, toutes ces impressions.

Voir est le sujet capté, ravi, ni vu ni connu.

Ni vu ni connu, je t'embrouille. Saisi : pris, captivé. Dessaisi : dépris, délivré. Les deux en un, mais pas "un" pour dire ou pour imager ce "deux en un", ce "un en deux". (Les deux yeux de quelqu'un, et les iris de Leiris.)

* * *

Il n'y aurait là (où donc ?) rien d'exceptionnel. Au contraire, la mesure intacte de la banalité même. Voilà comment ça part : on ne sait pas, et pourtant c'est à ce non-savoir qu'on reste accolé, accoté, accordé d'une manière inébranlable. Et c'est ainsi qu'on part : sûre aventure brouillonne, et désir vague que déjà son départ rend parfait, effilé comme une lame, comme l'âme de la momie, l'âme elle-même emmaillotée, bandelettée, bandée, à qui plus rien ne parvient, ni du monde, ni de la pensée, rien d'autre que la pression de la main, du désert ou de l'oeil qui la tient . . .

On sait seulement qu'il y eut impression, un instant, à l'instant. (Mais "il y eut" est faux : l'impression est toujours là, ou bien, on l'attend encore, on n'a d'elle que le pressentiment; le temps marche ici dans tous les sens à la fois, ou bien, il ne marche pas, temps seulement spatial, spacieux, et spasmodique. Ce temps n'est pas l'écoulement de la poudre dans le sablier, il est l'opercule de ce dernier, avec son double évasement.) Impression : quelque chose s'est pressé, quelque chose a pressé, imprimé une pression, un mouvement. Mais pas une image, ni une idée. Nous serions très loin de Proust : point de "madeleine", point de "pavés inégaux", point de reconstitution et point d'appropriation de la chose fugitive. (Et par conséquent, pas d'oeuvre d'art ?) Mais tout à l'envers : typographie sans type, imprimerie sans caractère, le Fugace à l'état pur. Impur, par conséquent, puisque ni posé dans la stabilité, ni échappé dans la fuite. Une impression qui ne se fait qu'à peine reconnaître comme impression. Qui déjà roule et coule dans cette autre chose, presque rien, le cours de ce qui n'a même pas de cours, de ce qui n'a pas d'histoire ni de mémoire. Un murmure évasif à travers d'innombrables interstices. Pas de date, pas de repère, encore moins de monument. Mais la chose, là, saisie *en tant qu'*elle est dessaisie.

La momie sans pyramide, simplement sèche au sable et au soleil spacieux. Les yeux et leurs iris sous les bandelettes, sous des bandes d'arc-en-ciel, comme le cou sous le ruban d'Olympia.

Olympe : plus de messages n'en parviennent. Cela ne manque pas. Les choses sont simplement à notre portée. Nous ramassons tranquillement les morceaux des dieux, avec des larmes claires qui nous lavent les yeux, qui nous cristallisent le regard pour l'autopsie fraternelle et conjugale. Ainsi faisait Isis des membres d'Osiris, et pour finir l'iris osé posé sur le dernier membre bandé.

La chose, là, saisie en tant que dessaisie—c'est-à-dire : en tant qu'on est dessaisi d'elle.

Que veut dire cet "en tant que?" C'est une question dont pas une philosophie ne s'acquitte. (La philosophie ne s'acquitte de rien : c'est sa grande misère, et c'est sa ressource irremplaçable.)

Il y a impression, et c'est parti. L'impression n'imprime rien (pas de type, pas de monogramme, pas d'empreinte, pas de caractère), mais l'impression presse quelque chose à même cette surface irisée, ce papier ou cet écran vaguement prêt à se mettre en oeuvre.

Mais si *vaguement* prêt . . . Il n'en reste déjà que l'écume—encore est-ce trop dire, il n'y a pas d'écume, pas de mousse. "Sillage" en dirait trop, lui aussi (de même que toute "trace"). Il n'y a que ce saisissement à l'instant dessaisi de soi, de toute possibilité de se saisir de soi. Une noce incestueuse, l'attouchement de la distance.

Un arc-en-ciel bandé à travers une pluie de larmes fines, presque finie.

C'est ainsi qu'on saisit le sable, qu'on est saisi et dessaisi de lui. La pupille, la petite poupée bandée, la momie ne contient que sable et sable, et grains de mica de l'iris. Le trou de l'oeil est le trou d'un sablier, que le temps retourne, de temps en temps, pour faire couler le sujet dans l'objet, ou le monde dans la conscience, puis les pensées dans les choses, et ainsi de suite, sans que cela même se remarque.

Banalité : l'impression qui soulève l'attention, un instant, une infime fraction d'attention *n'a aucun intérêt.* Rien à y attacher, rien à en retirer. On la passerait bien au compte incalculable et plat du "quotidien". Mais ce mot en dit beaucoup trop : il place des mesures et des évaluations, il réserve les belles, les grandes exceptions. Or voici ce dont il s'agit: *tout* est si quotidien que la catégorie de "quotidien" est vaine. Le quotidien passe toute mesure, toute raison du quotidien et de l'exceptionnel. Le quotidien détient et retient jalousement le dessaisissement de la saisie, il n'est fait que de ça, retournant le sablier.

On est touché pourtant, quelque chose a touché quelque point sensible.

(On joue, on ne joue pas, ici: c'est la règle du jeu. Tout cela est incroyablement, inestimablement sérieux. On se plaît au sérieux. Où l'on serre les yeux. Iris froncés, fleurs et vulves, vertus vulnérables, attouchements vulnéraires.)

Le quotidien, voici: il y a de très graves nouvelles dans l'air. La politique peut-être est au bord du gouffre; les plus proches sont atteints d'affections incurables; on est dans la déréliction. Mais une minute suit l'autre, et si l'on ne se tue pas, c'est qu'à quelque chose d'infime on demeure obstinément, non pas "attaché", comme on dit, mais exposé.

Cela ne peut se dire, et pourtant cela ne cesse d'être murmuré, et ce murmure fait l'idiome.

Un murmure comme du sable. Si on n'y prenait pas garde, le sable peu à peu ensevelirait tous les Sphinx et toutes les Pyramides. Ici, personne n'est commis à cette garde: aussi les énigmes, et les tombeaux, et les secrets, y sont-ils doucement effacés.

Effacés. Aux faces affaissées. Défaits. Décomposés. Délités. Dépecés. Pièce par pièce. Pulvérisés. Une particule après l'autre. *Partes extra partes*. Espacés. Extravasés. Déconstruits. Emiettés. Disséminés. Eparpillés. Emulsionnés. Emoussés. Dépliés. Repliés. Dépareillés. Encalminés. Calmement. Posément. Continûment. Obstinément.

* * *

Obstinément. Obstination. *Ostinato rigore*. On y reste, cela passe, cela franchit les exceptions. Cela fait voir la règle, et la renforce, et la conforte. Obstinément l'infime infirme les magnitudes tonitruantes. Qu'est-ce que cela prouve, va-t-on demander? Mais qui parle de prouver, et de prouver quoi? Les preuves, quand elles réussissent, ne montrent rien de plus que ceci: que la chose prouvée était donc là, hors de la preuve, et qu'on n'avait pas besoin de preuve pour y toucher. Iris voudrait dire ici : cette moirure à peine perceptible du n'avoir-pas-besoin-de-preuve.

Une évidence qui évide les yeux. Celle du sable.

Ces choses-là, dont on ne rend pas raison, n'offrent peut-être pas plus d'intérêt qu'elles n'autorisent de preuve. Mais quel intérêt y a-t-il à ce que cela ait "de l'intérêt"? Le même iris, à fleur d'oeil, insignifiant et superbe, rêve tout en surface de la momie sans rêve.

(La momie ne rêve pas : mais elle se déguise en rêve. Mômerie de la momie, enfantillage, carnaval.)

Celui qui regarde et qui raconte ses rêves (lui, il aime le faire, ou plutôt, il y tient, il y est tenu), sans intention et sans remplissement de signification, seulement pour l'impression, celui-là sait qu'il laisse filer entre ses doigts la poudre de l'improbable et de l'improuvable.

Alors, sa pupille est l'opercule intérieur d'un sablier qu'on peut retourner pour que le désert s'écoule dans l'intimité, ou l'intimité dans le désert, mesurant le quotidien.

* * *

Ce qui impressionne, et qui n'a pas d'intérêt : s'il était possible de trouver là une règle cardinale pour la "littérature" ? Alors, en effet, elle renoncerait aux Célébrations, aux Représentations, aux Inscriptions-et-Belles-Lettres et aux Pyramides-et-Sphinx-des-Textes. Elle se ferait sable, elle-même. En réalité, elle ne cesse pas de le faire. Mais cela se voit mal, cela se discerne à peine.

"Les Iris" pourrait être le nom d'une villa en bord de mer. Ce serait du banal un peu vulgaire. Il y aurait un vol, un crime, une disparition, tout un roman policier. On imagine, à côté, le voisin peu bienveillant, mais peut-être simplement aimant rire, qui baptise la sienne: "Osiris". Autre roman policier. Le voisin a quelque instruction supplémentaire. Mais cela même est vulgaire. On peut faire un peu plus, et prendre "Les Iris" pour nom d'une petite résidence en copropriété. A côté des Tulipes et des Pervenches. Quartier des Fleurs, nature et culture, police du roman.

Dès que la "culture" est détachée comme une peau, comme une pellicule, et montrée pour elle-même, miroitant sous quelques projecteurs, sous quelques chandelles de souper fin pour magazine, sa vulgarité est insupportable. Ainsi de la littérature, lorsqu'elle se propose "intéressante", ainsi de la philosophie, lorsqu'elle fait valoir l'importance, la profondeur et l'angoisse de ses pensées. Ainsi de l'art qui garantit qu'il est de l'art, et non pas rien.

Mais le "quotidien" n'est pas cultivé, même le "quotidien" du voisin cultivé qui a entendu parler des dieux Egyptiens, et qui sait ? qui a lu Plutarque. Le "quotidien" n'est donc pas non plus vulgaire. Mais sans doute, je l'ai dit, est-il déjà vulgaire de parler de "quotidien". Sans doute est-il vulgaire de vouloir catégoriser ce qui se passe, et que ça se passe. Aussi bien en énonçant "l'Histoire" qu'en disant "le quotidien". Mais par exemple, on dit "les iris", sans y penser, parce qu'il faut un titre et parce que, sans doute, on a reçu une impression—une espèce d'impression fugitive et futile : un sable de syllabe en "ris". Cela aurait pu venir de Ris-Orangis. La banlieue est le lieu du banal. Le banal est un lieu d'abandon. On s'abandonne aux impressions, au sablier des impressions.

C'est toujours singulier, c'est à chaque fois si singulier que chaque fois est l'exception, et que l'exception est la règle, et que la règle est en effet très régulière: l'existence est exceptionnelle.

L'existence est exceptionnelle, mais ça ne se voit pas. Et c'est ça qui est exceptionnel. Car tout se voit, tout est *phainomenon*, sauf *ça*. Ca s'écrit, mais même écrit, ça ne se voit pas, et ce n'est pas pour ça que c'est écrit.

Roman policier: pour quoi a-t-il écrit ? à qui profite le crime d'écrire ?

Si j'écris que l'existence—celle-ci, celle-là—est exceptionnelle, et banalement exceptionnelle, je ne l'écris pas pour en proposer la théorie, la considération ni la contemplation.

C'est écrit pour le temps perdu passé à écrire, quelques grammes d'existence, quelques instants d'insistance. . . .

C'est écrit pour les impressions qui ne laissent pas de trace, sinon qu'on s'est abandonné aux impressions. C'est écrit pour le sablier, sa chute minuscule et son retournement autour de l'axe.

Axe des iris, florilège axiologique: Augustin, Dante, Montaigne, Blake, Rousseau, Et Coetera.

Augustin:	"Ce que nous cherchons maintenant, c'est comment tu aimes la sagesse. Tu désires la voir, la posséder sans aucun voile, toute nue, si j'ose dire, avec des regards, des embrassements d'une parfaite chasteté."
Dante:	"Tel est celui qui voit en rêvant, et, le rêve fini, la passion imprimée, reste, et il n'a plus souvenir d'autre chose, tel je suis à présent, car presque toute cesse ma vision, et dans mon coeur coule encore la douceur qui naquit d'elle."

Montaigne: "J'ouvre les choses plus que je ne les descouvre."

Blake: "Les Filles des Séraphins conduisaient leurs clairs
troupeaux,
Hors la plus jeune qui, dans sa pâleur, cherchait la secrète
solitude,
Pour s'évanouir, telle la beauté matinale de son jour
mortel."

Rousseau: "Dominé par mes sens, quoi que je puisse faire, je n'ai
jamais su résister à leurs impressions, et, tant que l'objet
agit sur eux, je ne cesse d'en être affecté."

Et Coetera:

Mais au fond, personne, au fond, personne en particulier. L'in-
assouvi et inapaisable désir d'anonymat, la littérature de provenance
immense, infime, infirme, infinitésimale. Et coetera, et les membres
pulvérisés des dieux qui glissent entre les doigts d' Isis.

C'est-à-dire aussi bien: rien, nulle littérature. Au contraire, une
chasse incessante, une traque acharnée de toutes les littératures. C'est-
à-dire : de toutes les façons de croire qu'en mettant un panonceau "Les
Iris" on a transfiguré sa médiocre villa. Et de ces façons, il y a des
milliers. Des milliers de façons de représenter ou de figurer comment
en embarquant d'un très modeste port de pêche on trouvera la route des
épices, de l'or et de la soie, la route des Indes. Mais il n'existe pas
beaucoup de manières de retourner le sablier.

Il n'y a pas de route des Indes, même à partir des quais des plus
puissants Empires. Il y a le lent miroitement de la mer irisée, interminable, il y a du sel plein les yeux, des maladies, et on arrive ailleurs,
ou on n'arrive pas. Il n'y a pas de chemin vers l'or, la soie, ni vers le Soi,
vers soi, mais il y a ce long regard impressionnable que touchent chaque jour des millions d'oiseaux d'or, ou quelques aiguilles de pluie.

mars 1990

For Irizarry, Manhattan
(do not make the liaison, do not make the agreement either: nor the
phonetic liaison, as the French language here requires, nor the subject

agreement, as all thought [French or otherwise] requires. But do not take this double prohibition either as an introduction. Do not look for the key on one side or the other, even if it is clear that *les iris* is a plural of *l'iris*, in which the apostrophe elides an "e" to avoid the hiatus. Without this hiatus, here we would have *le iris*, from which only the capital letter of the proper name would be missing to give us finally the author who is the object of our attention today: "Leiris.")

Just tell yourself that it has begun [*c'est parti*]: there, we had to begin, and that's how it happened. We don't know why, or rather, it would be boring to know. The above is already boring enough to make us yawn. And a *hiatus* is nothing other than a kind of "yawning": the mouth gaping from the vocalization of the accumulated vowels. Language does not want to yawn. Language is constantly busy, bustling or fussing about, anxious or joyful: it does not let go of whomever it has a hold of. Leiris is held by language, day by day, and step by step, minutely, intimately, meticulously and preciously held.

There is no access to such a "holding." No one touches another's language. Idioms never meet one another. They are parallels, parataxes, hard particles. Each one proceeds, within its own idiocy, from a slight and irretrievable pressure exerted upon language by verbal expression. Each one emerges from an impression produced on language and by language, an inimitable impression in language's immense work of imitation. As fleeting as it is durable, as vague as it is precise. We get going, we speak under this impression, until adulthood and beyond. We have already got going, and we'll see what may come of it.

"We'll see": the iris surrounds the pupil. This is what we see through, they say. We see through the hole in which can be seen a little figurine (oneself, yourself leaning over an eye), and this hole, this operculum is surrounded by an iridescence, a glimmering, or shimmering of a rainbow, a goddess in fact, the goddess of sharing [*partage*] and of intimate nuances of color. A colored bow of peace, of an inaccessible peace around the agitation of the figurines. A goddess embracing the figurine, a shimmering surrounding the image.

(Iris is the messenger of the gods. But here it is a question of what happens when the gods no longer have any message to pass on. Nothing violent, nothing spectacular, no "death of the gods." Lighter, more sly as well perhaps, a simply everyday coming-and-going of signs, pulverized by insignificance—and yet it's like an interminable palaver with a stubborn little sphinx. It doesn't make a fuss, and yet it obstinately persists in haggling over inexpensive enigmas. There is no question of its playing Oedipus. No question of its blinding itself, yet "man" remains a puzzle, until adulthood and beyond. It's like an old habit you can't get rid of. Irises flutter about almost everywhere, carrying no-messages, but on the ground there is still that stubborn little sphinx.)

We'll see—that is, we may see nothing, or there may be nothing there to see (how can we tell?).

But that's how it got going, and how it always gets going. As when two looks meet momentarily. When a shimmering gleams for a moment. The moment is always too brief to hold on to. Or rather: it is only there in order to make felt that which cannot be grasped, that which one cannot hold on to: an impression. The vocation of a moment, that by which we call out to it—"Oh time, stop your flight!"—, is a letting go.

This letting go proves to be absolutely identical to a holding on to. The thing that took hold of me also let me go. The thing that took hold of me let itself go from me, leaving me more alone than it is imaginable to be alone. So alone that the only thing one knows about "oneself" is the solar spasm of a shimmering which has not even illuminated itself, or even thrown light upon itself. An iris caught by the void, caught as it envelops a pupil yawning (a hiatus) over nothing, over the solitude of its "subject." For, as we know, it never sees itself there. It never sees its vision. The sphinx has sand, shards of mica and the dust of old bones in its eyes.

A pupil bundled up in an iris: a minuscule Egyptian mummy in the heart of the eye. Variegated bandages tightly wound around this secret nothing: seeing.

You have to go and see for yourself. This is called an "autopsy," an *opsis* of the *auto*, seeing by oneself, seeing with one's own eyes, what we call seeing. A continuous autopsy of a tenuous existence, an anatomy of tiny details. All these things which take hold of us, which let go of us, all these impressions.

Seeing is the captured, ravished secret, nobody the wiser for it.

Nobody the wiser for it, I'm confusing you. Held: taken, captured. Let go: released, freed. The two in one, but not "one" to say or give an idea of this "two in one," this "one in two." (Someone's two eyes, and Leiris's irises.)

*   *   *

So there would be nothing exceptional here (but where?). On the contrary, the intact measure of banality itself. That's how it gets going: we don't know, and yet we remain unshakably attached to, close to, in harmony with this not-knowing. And that is how we get going: a decisive, muddled adventure, and a vague desire, which is already perfect as soon as it's on its way, sharpened like a blade [lame], like the mummy's soul [l'âme], the soul itself bundled up, bandaged, bound, nothing getting through to it any longer, nothing from the world nor from any thought, nothing but the pressure of a hand, of the desert or of the eye that beholds it . . .

We only know that there was an impression, for a moment, a moment ago. (But "there was" is wrong: the impression is still there, or rather, we are still waiting for it, we only have a premonition of it; here times goes forward in all directions at once, or rather time doesn't go, it is only spatial, spacious, and spasmodic. This time is not like sand running down in an hourglass, it is the operculum of the hourglass, with its double cup.) An impression: something was pressed for time, something pressed, imprinted a pressure, a movement. But not an image or an idea. We are a very long way from Proust: no "madeleine," no "uneven paving stones," no reconstitution or appropriation of the fleeting object. (And as a consequence, no work of art?). But quite the opposite: a typography without any type, a printing with no characters. Fugacity in its purest form, and consequently impure, since it is neither fixed in its stability, nor fugitive in its escape. An impression that hardly allows itself to be recognized as an impression, that is already moving and flowing into this other thing, almost nothing, the course of that which has no course, of that which has no history or memory. An elusive murmur through innumerable interstices. No date, no point of reference, much less any monument. But the thing, there, held *inasmuch as* it is let go.

A mummy without a pyramid, simply dry in the sand and the spacious sun. The eyes and their irises under the bandages, under the bands of the rainbow, like the neck under Olympia's ribbon.

Olympus: no more messages reach us from there. They are not missed. Things are simply within our grasp. We quietly pick up the pieces of the gods, with clear tears washing our eyes, crystallizing our gaze toward the fraternal and conjugal autopsy. This is what Isis did with Osiris's limbs, ending with the daring iris, resting upon the final bound limb.

The thing, there, held inasmuch as it is let go—that is: inasmuch as one is let go by the thing.

What does this "inasmuch as" mean? It is a question of which not a single philosophy has acquitted itself. (Philosophy acquits itself of nothing, that is its great poverty, and its irreplaceable asset resourcefulness.)

There's an impression, and it's gone [*c'est parti*]. The impression prints nothing (no type, no monogram, no imprint, no character), but it presses something into this iridescent surface, this paper or screen vaguely ready to be put to work [*se mettre en oeuvre*].

But so *vaguely** ready . . . there is already nothing left of it but the foam—even this is saying too much, there is no foam, no froth. To talk of a "wake" (or of any kind of "trace") would also be saying too much. There is only this taking hold, which at the same time lets go of itself, of any possibility of taking hold of oneself. An incestuous wedding, touching the distance.

A banded rainbow through a rain of fine, almost finite, tears.

This is how one takes hold of the sand, how one is taken hold of and let go from it. The pupil, the little bound figurine, the mummy only contains sand, and more sand, and the iris's grains of mica. The hole in the eye is the hole of an hourglass, that time turns over, from time to

*Play on *une vague* [a wave]—Translator's note.

time, to make the subject run into the object, or the world into the mind, and then thoughts into things, and so forth, without it ever being noticed.

Banality: the impression which arouses our attention, for a moment, a tiny fraction of our attention, *is of no interest*. There's nothing to attach to it, nothing to take away from it. One could well put it down to the incalculable flatness of the "everyday." But this word says too much: it measures and evaluates, it keeps fine, grand exceptions in reserve. Now, the fact is: *everything* is so everyday that the category of the "everyday" is worthless. The everyday goes beyond any measure, any reason determining the everyday and the exceptional. The everyday jealously holds on to and withholds the letting go of the hold, that is all it is made up of, turning over the hourglass.

Yet we are touched, something has touched some sensitive spot.

(We play, we don't play here: these are the rules of the game. This is all incredibly , inestimably serious. We enjoy the serious. When we squint [*l'on serre les yeux*].* Frowned irises, flowers and vulvae, vulnerable virtues, vulnerary touches.)

Here is the everyday: there is extremely serious news in the air. Politics is perhaps on the brink of an abyss: our nearest and dearest are suffering from incurable illnesses; we are in a state of dereliction. But one minute follows another, and if we don't kill ourselves, it is because we remains obstinately—not "attached," as they say—but exposed, to something quite tiny. It cannot be spoken, and yet it never stops being murmured, and this murmur makes an idiom.

A murmur like sand. If we didn't watch out, the sand would little by little bury all of the Sphinxes and all of the Pyramids. Here, no one is assigned this watch: so the enigmas, and the tombs, and the secrets, are all quietly effaced.

Effaced. With their faces collapsed. Undone. Decomposed. Partitioned. Dismembered. Bit by bit. Pulverized. One particle after another. *Partes extra partes*. Spaced out. Extravasated. Deconstructed.

*Play on *sérieux* and *serre les yeux*—Translator's note.

Dissipated. Disseminated. Scattered. Emulsified. Dulled. Unfolded. Folded back. Rendered incomplete. Immobilized [*Encalminés*]. Calmly. Deliberately. Continuously. Obstinately.

*   *   *

Obstinately. Obstinacy. *Ostinato rigore.* We remain there, it passes, it crosses the boundaries of exceptions. It allows us to see the rule, and reinforces it, and confirms it. The tiny thing obstinately invalidates thundering magnitudes. What does this prove, one might ask? But who said anything about proving, and proving what? Proofs, when they succeed, show nothing more than this: that the thing proved was indeed there, independent of proof, and that one didn't need any proof to touch it. This is the meaning of iris: this barely perceptible shimmering of that-which-needs-no-proof.

An evidence which hollows out [*évide*] the eyes. The evidence of sand.

These things, which one cannot account for, offer perhaps no more interest than they authorize proof. But what interest is there in the fact that it has "an interest?" The same iris, just above the surface of the eye [*à fleur d'oeil*], meaningless and splendid, dreams on the surface of the mummy without dreams.

(The mummy does not dream: but it is disguised as a dream. A mummy's mummery, a child's game, a carnival.)

The one who watches and recounts his dreams (he likes to do it, or rather he intends to, or is bound to do it [*il y tient, il y est tenu*]), without any purpose, and without filling them full of meaning, but just for the impression, he knows that he is letting the sands of the improbable and the unprovable run through his fingers. Thus his pupil is the inner operculum of an hourglass that one can turn over, so that the desert flows into intimacy, or intimacy into the desert, measuring the everyday.

*   *   *

What impresses, and is of no interest: and if it were possible to find in this a cardinal rule for "literature"? It would thus indeed renounce Celebrations, Representations, Inscription-and-Letters, and Pyramids-and-Sphinx-of-Texts. It would itself become sand. In reality, it never stops becoming sand. But this is difficult to see, this is hardly discernible.

"Les Iris" could be the name of a house by the sea. This would be a rather vulgar banality. There would be a theft, a crime, a disappearance, an entire detective novel. One can imagine the unfriendly next door neighbor (but perhaps he simply likes a good joke) naming his own house: "Osiris." Another detective novel. The neighbor is carrying out some other investigation. But that itself is vulgar. One could go a little further, and take "Les Iris" to be the name of a cooperative residence. Next to the Tulips and the periwinkles. The Flower district, nature and culture, the novel's detective.

As soon as "culture" is pulled off like a skin, like a film, and shown for its own sake, shimmering under a few spotlights, lit by a few fine dinner candles for a magazine, its vulgarity becomes intolerable. The same is true of literature, when it claims to be "interesting," and of philosophy, when it emphasizes the importance, the depth and the anguish of its thoughts. The same is true of art which guarantees that it is art, and not nothing.

But the "everyday" is not cultivated, not even the "everyday" of the cultivated neighbor who has heard of the Egyptian gods and (who knows?) who has read Plutarch. Nor is the "everyday" vulgar either. But it is no doubt already vulgar, as I've said, to talk of the "everyday." It is no doubt vulgar to want to categorize what happens, and the fact that it happens. Just as much in recounting "History" as in telling "the everyday." But we say "Les Iris," for example, without thinking about it, because we need a title, and no doubt because we received an impression—a kind of fleeting, futile impression. A sand syllable, "ris." It could have come from Ris-Orangis. The suburbs are the place where everything is banal. Banality is a place of abandonment. One abandons oneself to impressions, to the hourglass of impressions.

It is always singular, each time it is so singular that each time is the exception, and that the exception is the rule, and that the rule is in fact very regular: existence is exceptional.

Existence is exceptional, but this cannot be seen. And that is what is exceptional. For everything can be seen, everything is a *phainomenon*, except *that*. It can be written, but even when written, it cannot be seen, and that is not why it is written.

A detective novel: for what reason did he write? who profits from the crime of writing?

If I write that existence—this one, that one—is exceptional, and exceptional in a banal way, I do not write it to put it forward as a theory, a consideration or a reflexion.

It is written for the time wasted spent writing, a few grams of existence, a few moments of insistence. . . .

It is written for the impressions which leave no trace, except for the fact that one has abandoned oneself to impressions. It is written for the hourglass, the minuscule falling of its sand, and its turning around its axis.

An axis of irises, an axiological anthology: Augustine, Dante, Montaigne, Blake, Rousseau, Et cetera.

Augustine: "What we are looking for now is how you love wisdom. You long to see it, to possess it unveiled, quite naked, if I dare say so, with looks and embraces that are perfectly chaste."

Dante: "This is how a person is who sees while dreaming, and, the dream over, the passion imprinted, remains, and all other memory is gone, Such am I at present, for almost everything arrests my vision, and in my heart still flows the sweetness born of it."

Montaigne: "I disclose things more than I discover them."

Blake: "The Daughters of the Seraphim led round their sunny flocks,
All but the youngest, she in paleness sought the secret air.
To fade away like morning beauty from her mortal day."*

Rousseau: "Ruled by my senses, whatever I may do, I have never been able to resist their impressions, and as long as a given object acts upon my senses, I never stop being affected by these impressions."

Et cetera:

But basically, no one, basically, no one in particular. The unquenched and insatiable desire to be anonymous, literature with an immense, minuscule, infirm, infinitesimal source. Et cetera, and the pulverized limbs of the gods who slip through Isis's fingers.

That is to say, also: nothing, no literature. On the contrary, an eternal hunt, a relentless hounding of all literatures. That is to say: believing any way that by putting up a sign saying "Les Iris" you have transformed your mediocre house by the sea. And there are thousands of these ways. Thousands of ways of representing or figuring how, in setting sail from a very modest fishing port, one will find the route to spices, gold and silk, the route to the Indies. But there are not many ways of turning over an hourglass.

There is no route to the Indies, even departing from the quays of the most powerful Empires. There is the slow shimmering of the iridescent, interminable sea, there is an eyeful of sand, illnesses, and one arrives elsewhere, or one doesn't arrive at all. There is no path leading to the gold, to the silk [la soie], or even to the Self [le Soi], to oneself, but there is this long, impressionable look that is touched every day by millions of golden birds, or by a few darts of rain.

March 1990

—Translated by Michael Syrotinski

---

*William Blake *The Complete Poems* "The Book of Thel." (Harmondsworth: Penguin, 1977), 78.

DENIS HOLLIER

Poetry . . . up to Z*

NAME DROPPING: MONTAIGNE, ROUSSEAU, NERVAL

It required no less than Nerval's sponsorship for Montaigne's name to be slipped into *La Règle du jeu*. It happens down a sidepath in the gardens of Ermenonville where the author of *Aurélia* and *Pandora*—*Aurora*'s two sisters—used to stroll in search of forgetfulness of things past: "Where are the women who were our lovers? They are in the grave." Nerval's specter is soon accompanied by the much more palpable ghost of Rousseau, for it is there that the "solitary walker" died and was buried. It so happened that the park was designed to include a temple to philosophy and that this temple is dedicated "to Michel de Montaigne." Thus, in passing, in the course of a description, Leiris mentions him: name dropping; a name falls, for nothing.[1]

In fact it is Rousseau's tomb that is the real object of Leiris's description on the page of *Fibrilles* that evokes the park where, having sheltered the final days of the author of the *Confessions*, the Marquis de Girardin was to build a refuge for his ashes where they would remain until the Revolution called them to the Pantheon.

The evocation of the park at Ermenonville interrupts the meandering analysis that Leiris is making of one of his dreams just before the point where the text initiates a series of associations provoked by a

---

*First published as "La Poésie jusqu'à Z", in *L'Ire des vents*, nos. 3–4, (1981), special issue "Autour de Michel Leiris."

1. Michel Leiris, *Fibrilles, La Règle du jeu* (Paris: Gallimard, 1974), vol. 3, 58. Hereafter cited in the text.

YFS 81, *On Leiris*, ed. Blanchard, © 1992 by Yale University.

garden that is particularly difficult to bring into focus. The dreamer
turned analyst of his own dream no longer knows what level of reality
or irreality to endow it with. He dreamed it . . . but then it would be
necessary to determine if its intervention in the dream was its first
appearance, or if instead there hadn't already been a garden in his
memory that the dreamer was recalling, or, yet a third possibility, if—
rather than being present in the dream—the garden hadn't been tacitly
presupposed, an implicit but never verified presence that formed the
horizon of the dream sequence. On the other hand, Leiris wonders,
perhaps he is in the act, after the fact and pen in hand, of bodying it
forth in order to force it into a dream that can no longer speak for itself
to remind him that, originally, when he was dreaming instead of writing, it had unfolded without this horticultural baggage. Thus, before
beginning to unreel the associations elicited by the word *garden*, it's a
matter of determining as precisely as possible the exact status of the
prompt itself: where to locate this garden that he can no longer find in
the dream that had nonetheless conveyed it—secret garden, lost without having left any tracks, burrowed irretrievably into the depths of a
dream where it hides as though wanting to be forgotten forever.

Just at the moment of letting this phantom garden resonate, Leiris
stops, hesitates, wondering if he is not setting out to snatch from his
dream "a secret it does not have." (But how does one know whether a
secret is lacking or not?) These misgivings then begin the description
of the park at Ermenonville, which soon turns out to be the possessor
of its own sort of missing secret—the "site-specific" secret embedded
in a landscape that would serve as stage for a haunting. In fact, at the
end of a series of interlocking frames (the park itself, the lake, the
island, the circle of poplars), the reader is led to the marble tomb
"where, as Nerval said, *Rousseau's ashes are missing*".[2]

The setting of Rousseau's empty tomb is not introduced by Leiris
for its sole thematic value, as the first variation on the garden theme,
but for the way it works scenographically. It repeats the dream scene
that has elicited it. Rousseau's remains are not there in the garden they
haunt, just as the phantom garden is not there in the dream evoking it.
Cenotaph and empty dream: this scenography is *cenography*. It looks
like nothing. The scene is deserted. How far can a text go? It goes just
far enough not to say where it comes from. Nor where it is going. Not
one step farther. The description accumulates endless baroque ellipses

2. The italics are Leiris's: he is quoting Nerval.

around whatever it is circling, endlessly expanding upon the eclipse of its center. Its sole excuse for existence is that whatever it revolves around, whatever supports it, is lacking. Over and over it relentlessly repeats that its core has been emptied. At the heart of the text lies what Leiris often deplores about himself, "a real lack of heart."

(At the beginning of *L'Age d'homme*, Leiris recounts his "first actual contact with the notion of infinity":[3] it was induced by the label on a box of cocoa, on which there was a picture of a Dutch woman carrying a tray on which there was an identical box of cocoa on whose label there was, consequently, a picture of the same Dutch woman who . . . etc., ad infinitum. The memories surrounding this page insert this first contact with the notion of infinity in a series of childhood fantasies concerning the *contents* of the notion of person (what does it mean, in terms of spatial organization, to have a soul? How do babies come out of their mothers' bellies?) The notion of infinity, introduced by the Dutch woman of childhood breakfasts, reappears in *Fibrilles* with Rousseau's empty tomb, a tomb which, in fact, does not merely reproduce the structure of the dream with the unretrievable garden, but, through some unaccountable anticipation, ends up reproducing a miniature of the book to come in which it will figure. Leiris attempts suicide in the middle of *Fibrilles*. At the center of his book, the author buries himself, goes down into a tomb which, as the cenographic economy requires, will remain empty. For the descent to be central, it has to be abortive, at the same time missed and missing. *Fibrilles* remains, the cenotaph deprived of the ashes it was meant to have as its hearth— living, nameless ashes, *vivantes cendres innommées*, the author's remains. At Rousseau's tomb, before even beginning to exist, *Fibrilles* begins its infinite regression in the tomb where it is missing, regressing to emptiness, to infinity. The first poem Leiris ever published had as its title, "Nothing is ever ending.")

As for Montaigne, a homologous ring runs through the *Essais*, where it marks a similar empty space, dug between *centre* and *cendre*—between center and ashes. Here again, a cenographic writing, a writing that nothing fulfills and yet that is the utter fulfilment of writing, creates a similar void. The first project for the *Essais* revolved around a text that Montaigne had planned to put at the center of his

3. Michel Leiris, *L'Age d'homme*, translated by Richard Howard as *Manhood. A Journey from Childhood into the Fierce Order of Virility* (New York: Grossman, 1963), 130. All long quotations from *L'Age d'homme* follow Howard's translation. Hereafter cited in the text.

book even though he had not written it: La Boétie's *Discours de la servitude volontaire* was to be the most voluminous citation in a work that, nonetheless, did not lack citation. So Montaigne introduces himself—by introducing the remains of his alter ego. He uses someone else's text for his own authorization, only becoming an author once augmented by this first volume of works by his ex-*moitié*. For political reasons, he later replaced the *Discours* with a series of twenty-nine sonnets by La Boétie, a doubly foreign body with the *Essais;* because, on the one hand, they were not written by the person signing the book in which they appear, and on the other, it is a poetic work inserted as a heterogeneous center into the heart of a text written, prosaically, in the language of everyday.

Montaigne started writing—and he went as far as having this incribed on the walls of his library—in reaction to the loss of this friend for whom the earliest draft of the *Essais* was intended as a sort of tomb. The final shape of the volume would make this tomb strangely resemble Rousseau's tomb in the park at Ermenonville: Montaigne literally clears them out. No one knows why, but he gets rid of his dead friend's sonnets. In their place—the place which remains central, but which they do not occupy, and with the title still proclaiming a presence they do not provide ("Twenty-Nine Sonnets by Etienne de La Boétie")—there are only the words "These verses may be seen elsewhere." Rousseau's ashes may be seen elsewhere as well—in the Pantheon. No one has yet managed to locate the exact place to which Montaigne was sending readers to see his friend's poems. *A demain la poésie.* Poetry can wait. Autobiographical discourse dismisses poetic writing, and the poems retreat before their introduction. First an orderly retreat, then they desert.

What I would like to suggest is that similarly, throughout his autobiographical works, Leiris continually says a mournful goodbye to poetry, encircling it as it retreats, tracking its absence, lamenting what he calls in *Frêle bruit* "the silence of the sibyl's lair: the deserted chair of the oracle whose voice is amputated".[4] Orpheus sang of Euridyce's disappearance, Leiris sings of the loss of this voice, the "voice off" singing its great aria. Just as Montaigne bids farewell to his double, Leiris says goodby to the poet he will never become. *La Règle du jeu:* Cenotaph to Michel Leiris, Poet.

One final word about Montaigne: the words with which, in the

---

4. Michel Leiris, *Frêle bruit La Règle du jeu.* (Paris: Gallimard, 1976), vol. 4, 348. Hereafter cited in the text.

chapter "On Friendship," he commends the poems of his former alter-ego, the poet, indicate that there is a temperamental incompatibility making it impossible for poetry and autobiography to set up house together, and condemning them in advance to divorce. There can be no such thing as the memoirs of a poet if it is true that the words of a poem are always words without memory, *mots sans mémoires*.[5] It is, precisely, a question of housekeeping, a certain way writing has of getting organized and husbanded. Montaigne said, in praise of La Boétie's sonnets, that he wrote them "en sa plus verte jeunesse," in the flush of youth. They demonstrate a fire, an "ardor" not to be found in the later poems he wrote "for his wife" that have an air, Montaigne writes, of "I don't know what marital frigidity." In the third book of the *Essais*, in the chapter "On some lines in Virgil," he expressed his astonishment at finding in the *Aeneid* a "very tender" picture of a "marital Venus." The love of poetry makes a bad marriage with the prose of legitimate unions.

REVOCATIONS

> Tone is not the voice of the writer, but the intimacy of silence he imposes upon speech.
> —Maurice Blanchot

It is vocation that makes a poet: he has been called by the only name to which he answers; he is marked.

There was nothing demanded of Leiris, and his autobiography continually returns to the spot at which this label "Poet" is missing—the mark that would have authorized this text endlessly remarking its absence. Leiris had no vocation, this is where all his work begins, this is his sticking point.

The truth is that Leiris, at about the age of ten, experienced a sense that he was not just called but truly chosen by a vocation. For a second an angel of glory descended upon him in an annunciation that calls to mind the triumphant euphoria that Raymond Roussel described to

5. Both *Mots sans mémoire* and *Vivantes cendres innommées* are collections of poems by Leiris.

Janet, or perhaps the Proustian experience of the past regained, except that for Leiris the experience was preliterary, just barely linguistic, a child's adventure. In *Fibrilles*, he recounts how he was overcome by this feeling (*Fibrilles*, 246). The scene took place at Heist-sur-Mer in Belgium, at the end of the family vacation. They were playing a game in which he had to leave the living room while the two left behind could choose a card together, without his knowing which one it was. They chose one (or at least he thought they did), and called him back. He had to try and find the right one among all the others spread out on the table. Really, however, while he was gone, they had decided to pretend that the card he picked when he came back—no matter what it was— was the one they had chosen. And so he chose correctly once, twice, and over and over again, until quite naturally he came to the obvious conclusion: he had a gift for divination that he had never before had a chance to exhibit, or even to suspect, which henceforth would set him off from ordinary mortals, among the visionary elite. Leiris tells this incident obviously because of the cruel let-down that inevitably followed when he was shown how the trick worked. Later he made another connection: "Thinking about my experience at Heist-sur-Mer when I believed I had a gift that would have set me oddly apart from the ordinary, I have long wondered about the extent to which I was motivated by a drive not unlike this childish pride, when I became a young man, and not really knowing what to do with myself, I wanted *to be a poet*" (*Fibrilles*, 248). Which, as a vocation, was only a trap, a dangerous back alley. He thought he was possessed, but really was just plain, splendidly, *had*. To have been endowed with the gift of gifts, that of prophecy and clairvoyance, should have made him an oracle. But instead the "gift" left only a sad taste of ashes in the wake of its ridiculously false appearance of a present.

A related episode in the chapter "Dimanche" in *Biffures*, opens the section describing the choice of career. This time the setting is a church. The boy who would later define himself as "a specialist in confession" was leaving the confessional when the vicar called him and took him aside to say, "My little Michel, I have watched you closely: I see you have signs of the vocation, I am sure you would make a very good priest."[6] Of course, "little" Michel was bound to be affected as he grew up by the signs that this proselytizing priest-recruiter at-

6. Michel Leiris, "Dimanche," *Biffures La Règle du jeu* (Paris: Gallimard, 1948), vol. 1, 203.

tached to him. With his ego so swollen, a fit of megalomaniacal pride very nearly convinced him that he was "a kind of chosen person." As in the episode at Heist, this was followed by the detumescence of a return to reality. But the narrator did not wait for a specialist in ecclesiastical practices to demystify him concerning these so-called signs before refusing the future to which they were an invitation. Real or not, he immediately decided to avoid this vocation, and the reason invoked for this refusal is worth a pause: "there was an obligation, for those who took holy orders, to be chaste and correlatively, marriage was forbidden."

Here we must return again to *L'Age d'homme*—particularly its final chapters, which no longer have anything much to do with the autobiographer's childhood. As far as both life and writing are concerned, the autobiography is engendered and resolved here. These chapters are dominated by the dark figure of Holofernes which looms over vocation and marriage as they dance back and forth in a tragi-comic ballet. Because, though we saw the child, Leiris, refuse an alleged vocation that would have condemned him to virginity and celibacy, in *L'Age d'homme*, we find him some ten years later, presenting himself—immediately after describing himself as a disoriented bachelor "tempted by nothing," and "destined for nothing"—as the possessor "more even than of a vocation, of a *destiny*," in this case the destiny of celibacy, chastity and "absolute purity" ("and lack of satisfaction") that is the lot of those who live the poet's existence. The reason for this turnaround? He wants to escape marriage. "I meditated on Gobineau's fable," he wrote," (one of the *Nouvelles asiatiques*) of the initiate to whom an illustrious thaumaturge is about to reveal the ultimate magic secret, but who loses everything on the threshold of discovery because he turns back when his wife who saw herself being abandoned, follows and calls to him" (*Manhood,* 130). (On the threshold of discovery—a find, a stroke of genius—just as he was about to learn the last word of the whole thing, the final letter, the omega, just as he was about to reach the *Z*, scarcely a hair's breadth from seeing the underside of the cards, the thing hiding behind the veil, etc. And that was the precise moment someone had to call him! The precise moment someone had to make him see that his name was written on the marital calling! Of course, in Gobineau's tale, according to Leiris's summary, the catastrophe is not because the wife follows and calls the initiate, but rather because the initiate responds to his name and lets himself be distracted by the call. He is already torn between bifurcating desires that condemn him to digression and distraction).

Gobineau's fable is mentioned as a sort of conclusion to a liaison Leiris has just broken off. He considers its lesson: one must choose between work and life. To have access to the ultimate revelations of poetry, one must renounce marriage ("being married would not have fit with my situation as a poet.") And moreover . . . he intends to renounce even sexuality. One might even suspect that this poetic vocation had miraculously sprung up just to spare him sexual relations. In fact it occurred at the period of his first liaison, when Leiris started being involved in what Rousseau called the "women's dwelling," (which he also described as not agreeing with him). It is from this time, he writes, that "date my first aspirations toward poetry, which appeared to me strictly speaking, as a refuge, a way of finding once more an enclosed area that was mine alone, in which my partner would have no need to interfere."

There is a touch of the Medusa weaving through the fabric of *L'Age d'homme,* like the thread of a fugue that rises again and again to the surface. The legendary *Raft of the Medusa* provides the title to the last chapter, and in the first, entitled "Tragiques," her figure is connected with a character in Offenbach's opera *The Tales of Hoffmann.* In an epigraph borrowed from Goethe's *Faust* (Nerval's translation, of course) we have just seen Mephistopheles warning his protégé against something that, had it been the right moment, could have become an example of the vampire at noon figure,—the specter of Marguerite with her throat cut. Then Mephistopheles speaks: "That rigid stare would 'thick man's blood with cold' and almost turn it into stone. Haven't you heard about Medusa?" Almost into stone. If one takes literally the passage in which Leiris connects his poetic calling with "a symbolic attempt at *mineralization*," this might be expressed in his words as "into a poet," or almost. Moreover, he clarifies this mineralization as "a defense-reaction against my inner weakness and the collapse by which I felt myself threatened; I longed for some kind of armor, seeking to achieve in my external persona the same ideal of stiffness and rigidity which I pursued poetically" (*Manhood,* 127). It is not desire, but terror that erects men when confronted with women, says Freud. As if man were paralyzed in front of the other's cut. The sun also rises, but Aurora (Muse and Medusa) now dawns with her name spelled "Horror."

What lesson is there in Gobineau's fable? Even more, where and how should it be remembered? What did Leiris think he was being warned against? The question becomes even more important when all this bachelor's poetic rigor is immediately followed ("I relaxed") by a matrimonial limpness presented in *L'Age d'homme* as a "half betrayal" and in *Fibrilles* as a "double betrayal." The amount of betrayal is not very important. This is not the first time that Leiris renounces a vow of chastity in order to be able to get married. As for the poetic calling—though he may have betrayed it by this marriage, it scarcely existed before his betrayal.

It may seem excessive to describe this as "going limp," but in the words of the author himself, ever since this event—that is, his marriage—he felt himself "still less than Holofernes's head."

AND MY ALL WILL NEVER COME TO PASS

> Grail whose name does not end but remains in the air, stretching into invisible currents.
>
> —Michel Leiris

The difference between the real and imaginary should not be negotiable.

Despite first appearances, the pages of *L'Age d'homme* in which the author reports (taking a certain guilty pleasure in his guilt) the circumstances of his marriage are not merely anecdotal. Nor is it sufficient simply to consider these pages as providing a sort of psychological interest as clinical records, putting one in a position to grasp the complicated maneuvers of a masochism ready to confess to anything. Going beyond the equivocal pleasure of confession, these pages are important because they stage the *genotext* of the autobiography.

Both in his life and in his work, Leiris's marriage constitutes the realistic turning point—one that involves his conversion to autobiographical writing. It is probably not possible to espouse reality. Close up it turns out to be just as much a phantom as the Africa into which this realism led him, (providing him at the same time with a second vocation). However, married he must leave "the country of his dreams," as a text from his earlier surrealist period had called it.

Though formerly he "accorded a preponderant importance to the *imaginary*" (*Manhood*, 126), and wanted "to escape reality," the auto-biographical/conjugal device cuts right through his life, slicing it in two. —On one side lies the imaginary with its dreams and its stock of poetry, but this is now behind him. Before him lies reality—to come. Between the two is the nonnegotiable frontier described in the first sentence of *L'Age d'homme:* "I have just reached the age of thirty-four, life's midpoint" (*Manhood*, 3). The first half was spent chasing after his dreams; the second half will be devoted to the pursuit of reality. A later preface added in 1946, just after the war, for a new edition of *L'Age d'homme*, recalls the esthetic and moral decision that had presided over its writing: the "predilection for realism" and the rejection of any "deceptive compromise between real facts and the products of imagination."

This marriage, therefore, is not simply an anecdote—either senti-mental or cynical—to be thrown out of the text and dumped into a biographical chapter in some study on Leiris. It is not one of the events experienced by the author of *La Règle du jeu*, but rather the birthplace of this author. It is the place, of union and divorce, where henceforth Leiris's life and work—identical at the same time that they are rival—advance and stagnate concurrently, in step. Impatient and incompati-ble, though they conjoin and constrain each other, both are irre-pressible.

The journey to the end of unreality recounted in *L'Age d'homme* ends with an awakening; it is enunciated as the marriage, and its enunciation is autobiography—the text of *L'Age d'homme* itself. "Dreaming every night, noting down my dreams, considering some of them to be revelations whose metaphysical meaning I had to discover, lining them up end to end in sequence so I could decipher their mean-ing better, thus deriving little stories from them, I woke up screaming almost every night" (*Manhood*,). Should one mention here Lacan's symbolic? Conjugality permits an escape from *idios cosmos*. It makes an opening into the unsharability of the dream world; it tolls the vespers for dreams. And at the same time, it negotiates this passage to reality through a soundless awakening. A miniature version of this passage serves as the conclusion to several of the dreams told in *Nuits sans nuit:* 8–9 October 1933: "but *Z* . . . awoke me, warning me that I was about to scream"; 29–30 Sept. 1957: "*Z*. (awakened from real sleep by my starting to scream) spoke to me." *La Règle du jeu*, whose first volume is dedicated to this same awakener—"*Z*"—shows us a simi-

larly repressed cry in its very first chapter: ". . . Reusement!" is lost to
be regained as "Heureusement!"

The Collège of Sociology rebelled against a life composed entirely
of daily humdrum. They had to put an end to this, to escape it. Exceptions to the rule of everyday banality, things escaping the rule of the
ordinary, they called "the Sacred." Leiris made an important contribution to the Collège, and in his contribution one may read his reserva-
tions concerning the Collège's project. All this is summed up power-
fully in the wording of his title, "The Sacred in Everyday Life." He will
deal in polemical inclusion rather than simple antagonism. At the end
of the poem "Dichter's Beruf," Hölderlin speaks of man as waiting "for
succor from the lack of God." It must be understood that, just as Rousseau's ashes are absent from the park at Ermenonville, the sacred it
absent from, or to put it more strongly, the sacred is absent *in* everyday
life. It is the day that days lack, the lack one notices as days go by. The
blindspot where everyday life is eclipsed, goes bad, is caught lacking:
the sacred in everyday life, days with no day. "Tragique," a poem in
Haut Mal began on just such a split: "Between loves and *love*": Loves
without love. Divorce is always the multiplication of a plural deprived
of the singular—the one thing called for. *Nuits sans nuit, Jours sans
jour.* Nights with no night, Days with no day: the singular is lacking in
everyday life. In Latin, *divortium* means bifurcation as well: *divortium
itinerum* is distraction from the one. Beatrice was my distraction.
Distraction was my Beatrice.

La Règle du jeu is ruled by the same logic throughout. Poetry is
literally reported missing by autobiographical prose. But, like
Höderlin in the absence of the gods, Leiris's prose finds mourning for
poetry to be a surprising resource for increasing poetic build. For Mallarmé, poetry was the power of negation driving things to retreat before
their absence, making them give way and shrink before their lack:
poetry produces for each thing the place where it is missing. Autobiography, precisely in setting itself up as the tomb of poetry, becomes
the space where poetry itself—the object this time of poetical operation—is gone, replaced by its vibrating quasi disappearance. But one
would have to say that rather than infinitely retreating into multiply-
ing abysses, poetry seems to founder. It is hurt by the lack. This is not
poetry within poetry, but poetry with no poetry, poems without a
poem. The singular is lacking—to the bitter end.

La Règle du jeu! The rule too is missing from the game whose title
it provides. The author has played the game—but without the rule.

This was supposed to be produced in *Fibules*, which earlier volumes had announced would conclude the project, coming to "even everything out." (And if everything is even there is somehow no game.) It was to give away the "final secret"—the "relentlessly coveted grail," as in some *Nouvelle asiatique* by Gobineau. It ends up, as we know, not being there at the end of the game. *La Règle du jeu* does not lead to some remembered and recovered time. Instead, toward the end of *Fibrilles*, there are a few instructions laid out: rules with no rule. But didn't *Fibules* have to go lacking? Wasn't it, because of the plural of its title, doomed to lack that one point where scattered perceptions of earlier volumes could be collected, the point that would hold together their plurality under its authority? Why should it take several fibulae to fasten a single rule? But at the very place where these *Fibules* are lacking, there is *Frêle bruit*—the one and only singular title of the series it resolves. Just as unique, just as singular as a sound with no message: "thin noise," "fragile sound," which nevertheless, in "Mors" already had just one thing to say—and "this unique thing it said was that it was *unique*." But this one singular is doomed to dispersal: there at the place where everything was supposed to even out, is "only the dispersing, the disparate and the incoherent." *Frêle bruit:* bursts of singularity, an archipelago of the unique.

> My first: one seeks a grail that will be everything for you. But one could go on forever uttering it: one never comes to the last letter of the last word.
>
> My second: autobiography is the art of attaining one's end. But with distraction: one touches it, moves it, and never finds it again.
>
> My third: by way of exit, merely to mark time (a negative marker), casually, as if nothing were going on: "taken from Dublin, the front door of 7 Eccles Street where Leopold Bloom lived, a Georgian door, I think, that—moved now to the first floor of Bailey's bar where it is inside next to the toilets—closes nothing and opens onto nothing." [*Frêle bruit*, 334]

POSTSCRIPT: One extra, one final rhyme to this sort of backwards *abc* and its charade in *z:* I call to the stand, after the fact, one further absence: "on the credenzas, in the empty room, no ptyx." Was it, really, necessary to go to Paris to find this out? Certain absences go without saying: one can miss them just by wanting to verify them. They condemn us to always being a step behind them. Just the same, how could the expression "where Rousseau's ashes are missing" not be missing from the text by Nerval from which Leiris took it? There's no lack of lack at the source. This quote, of course, is only literally missing. The spirit is there and Leiris was quoting from memory. As for the page in *Fibrilles* where the description of the park at Ermenonville leads to this borrowing with no source, Leiris tells me that he recalls having written it while thinking of the advertising wrapped around Sartre's *L'Etre et le néant* when it was published. Printed on the band were the words: "What counts in a vase, is the empty space in the center."

—Translated by Betsy Wing

LEAH D. HEWITT

Between Movements: Leiris
in Literary History

To read the autobiographical works of Michel Leiris is to partake of the strangely elating malaise of the interval, like a person trying to sit between chairs without crashing to the floor.[1] Balancing on the invisible edges between fact and fiction, between genres (autobiography being a thoroughly "mixed and transgressive genre"),[2] between deliberate choices and fortuitous discoveries—to name only a few of its paired opposites—Leiris's four volumes of autobiography, La Règle du jeu, consistently try to juggle all at once the principles of autobiography, poetry, ethics, and personal experience.[3] To break down the barrier between life and art is perhaps Leiris's most cherished literary aspiration as he focuses on the potential of language, its games, and its powers beyond Cartesian logic, without, however, forsaking the social responsibilities it requires of its users. Leiris's readers quickly learn that his explorations in language harbor a fundamental ambivalence

1. Thinking that I was the first to describe Leiris's situation with this phrase, I find that in a 1976 review article of Frêle bruit (volume four of La Règle du jeu), the caption below a photograph of Leiris reads: "Toujours assis entre deux chaises," [Always seated between two chairs]. See: Claude Roy, "Un minutieux bourreau de soi-même," Nouvel Observateur (23 February, 1976), 58. Once a work has been identified in a note, subsequent references will be given in the essay with the corresponding page number. Unless noted otherwise, translations from the French are my own.

2. Mary Jacobus, "The Law of/and Gender: Genre Theory and the Prelude," Diacritics 14:4 (1984): 50.

3. Michel Leiris, La Règle du jeu (Paris: Gallimard: vol. 1 Biffures 1948, rpt., 1968; vol. 2 Fourbis, 1955; vol. 3 Fibrilles, 1966; vol. 4 Frêle bruit, 1976). See also Leiris's autobiographical essays (also published by Gallimard): Le Ruban au cou d'Olympia, 1981; Langage tangage ou ce que les mots me disent, 1985; A Cor et à cri, 1988.

YFS 81, On Leiris, ed. Blanchard, © 1992 by Yale University.

toward their object, "this language both adored and abhorred" (*Langage tangage*, 146). Readers must therefore relinquish any hope of identifying a univocal truth about, or a successful synthesis of, the subject's life in language. Following in the steps of the writer, we are invited to lose our footing in an ongoing game whose aim would be to determine/proclaim the force of literature in life and of life in literature.[4] As Michel Butor says of Leiris: "He makes us, whether we like it or not, collaborators of his attempt. . . ."[5]

In many ways, Leiris's autobiographical works are, no doubt, postmodern *avant la lettre,* for Leiris questions (as early as the 1930s and 1940s) the status of writing in ways that are commensurate with the concerns of deconstruction and more generally, poststructuralism.[6] If one takes postmodern writing to be "open, playful, optative, provisional, (open in time as well as in structure or space), disjunctive, or indeterminate . . . a discourse of ironies and fragments," but also one of "ubiquitous interactions, immanent codes . . . ,"[7] then *La Règle du jeu* is probably the most probing incarnation in twentieth-century France of its autobiographical dimensions.

But such a sweeping statement is too vast to account for Leiris's specific concerns or his "place"—between movements—in literary history. What makes his autobiography so emblematic of modern French literature (from around World War II on) is that he brings out, via the peculiar tensions inherent in autobiography, the concerns of the varying literary movements of his time: neither a "pure" representative of existentialist literature, nor the embodiment of the modernist writer (in the way one sometimes speaks of the New Novelists), Leiris does manage to articulate in autobiography borders with both as he tries to link the free play of linguistic experimentation and sociopolitical commitment.[8] The autobiographical genre is a particu-

4. Leiris wrote in the 1940s that his goal consisted of finding the moments in his past when he was about to "lose his footing." See: *Biffures,* 126.
5. Michel Butor, "Une autobiographie dialectique," in *Répertoire* 1 (Paris: Editions de Minuit, 1960), 268.
6. In his provocative study, *Politics, Writing, Mutilation: The Cases of Bataille, Blanchot, Roussel, Leiris, and Ponge* (Minneapolis: University of Minnesota Press, 1985), Allan Stoekl aptly brings out important connections between the writers of his title and poststructuralists Jacques Derrida, Michel Foucault, and Gilles Deleuze.
7. Ihab Hassan, *The Postmodern Turn: Essays in Postmodern Theory and Culture* (Columbus, OH: Ohio State University Press, 1987), 93–94.
8. This kind of link was, no doubt, already a concern of the surrealists in the 1920s and Leiris's autobiography bears very tangible traces of his surrealist days.

larly apt venue for addressing such questions because its marginal status in literary canons compels one to rethink its specificity, and because for Leiris autobiography retains referential concerns (of veracity, honesty) despite its fictive and artistic attributes.

Leiris posits both sociohistorical "engagement" and the magic of poetry as the (elusive) referents of his life-writing. In this context, the exemplarity of his endeavor would consist in dramatizing not only the rift but the interaction between existentialism and the New Novel through the issue of referentiality. His autobiography inquires into the genre's definition and rules—as a self-representation of writing (so common in the New Novel), while it never renounces the search for a personal ethic of writing. In what follows, I would like to review a few of the ways Leiris's autobiography meets up with these two literary currents of our time.

LEIRIS AND SARTREAN COMMITMENT

According to most critics, Leiris's autobiographical works would appear altogether objectionable to the Sartrean existentialist of the '40s or '50s.[9] It is certainly true enough that Leiris's passion for poetry and for language's purely pleasurable turns and twists, when words take on a life of their own instead of merely transmitting a message, runs counter to Sartre's more functional, politicized views of language. For some, Leiris's collaboration with Sartre on the original editorial board of *Les Temps modernes* in the 1940s was a "mutilation" of Leiris's own literary propensities. Anna Boschetti argues that because of the existentialist influence, Leiris's poetic and ethnographical production was almost nonexistent from the postwar period to the 1960s: instead, Leiris wrote autobiographical pieces which were more adaptable to the purposes of the existentialists' journal.[10] In either scenario, Leiris and the existentialists are considered very ill-matched in the literary arena.

And yet, the interactions are perhaps less awkward or less noxious for Leiris than one might think. Instead of being hostage to his ties to Sartre or existentialism, he actually alters existential precepts for his

9. Allan Stoekl makes this point in *Politics, Writing, Mutilation*, xv. Leiris's attraction to the seductions of poetic play corresponds to Georges Bataille's notion of expenditure, which Stoekl describes as "the human tendency to expend rather than conserve," as opposed to the "desire for a just, rationalized society."

10. Anna Boschetti, *Sartre et "les Temps modernes"*, (Paris: Editions de Minuit, 1985), 237–38. "Mutilation" is Boschetti's word.

own ends. It should first be noted that Leiris did write (and publish)
some poems and several ethnographical essays during the time he
worked with the *Temps modernes* group in the postwar years, but he
published most of them in other journals and books.[11] And although
Leiris himself laments his lack of poetic writing in the first volume of
La Règle du jeu,[12] at a time when he had become friends with Sartre,
the makeshift choice of autobiographical writing (in lieu of poetry) is
one that he had already made in the 1930s in response to what Leiris
described as a fundamental incompatibility between the "total exi-
gency" of poetry and the routine of an "ordered life" (*Biffures*, 237).
Leiris had turned to autobiographical writing (journal, self-portrait . . .) as a necessary stopgap, "in order to defend himself against the
idea of death" (*Biffures*, 238), well before he met Sartre and de Beauvoir.[13]

Although Leiris may not have influenced Sartre's and de Beauvoir's
taste in poetry,[14] his self-portrait, *L'Age d'homme* (first published in
1939), turns out to be exemplary for both of them. In *La Force des
choses*, de Beauvoir associates the beginnings of her autobiographical
project with having read Leiris: ". . . I felt like speaking about myself. I
liked *L'Age d'homme* by Leiris; I had a taste for martyr-essays in which
one explains oneself without excuses (vol. 1, 136). And Sartre also
suggests a connection between the (eventual) genesis of his own self-
portrait, *Les Mots*, and *L'Age d'homme*. In his journal of 1939 he explains: "It took the war and then the convergence of several new disci-

11. For references to Leiris's poetic and ethnographical publications during the
postwar years, see: Louis Yvert, "Bibliographie des écrits de Michel Leiris," *Bulletin du
Bibliophile*, 1 (1974): 8–49, and 3 (1974): 271–314. Most of the poems written and
published during the postwar years were republished in *Haut mal, suivi de Autres
Lancers* (Paris: Gallimard, 1969). Leiris's ethnographical publications during the period
are in fact rather numerous.
12. *Biffures*, 237: "I write hardly any poems anymore and no more imagined stories. . . ." In *Fourbis*, 65, Leiris says that it is "the alarms of our era" that distance him
from poetry (rather than his contact with existentialism). It should nevertheless be
pointed out that Leiris's autobiographical enterprise is itself a highly poetic endeavor.
13. In discussing *L'Age d'homme*, Denis Hollier locates this choice in Leiris's work
at the time of Leiris's marriage in the 1920s. See: "La Poésie jusqu'à Z," in *L'Ire des vents*
3–4 (1981): 141–54, and in this issue, 67, 70–73. I think it could easily be argued that
Leiris's most significant, innovative contribution to literature is his poetics of autobiographical writing rather than his poetry.
14. Concerning Leiris's participation in *Les Temps modernes*, Simone de Beauvoir
notes: "Leiris was in charge of poetry and our tastes seldom coincided." See: *La Force
des choses*, (Paris: Gallimard, 1963), vol. 1, 73. (Cited in *Sartre et "les Temps modernes"*, 238.)

plines (phenomenology, psychoanalysis, sociology), as well as the reading of *L'Age d'homme,* to incite me to draw up a portrait of myself."[15] Leiris's self-portrait, which focuses on the author's private mythology as it articulates sexual obsessions and feelings of inadequacy is, for Sartre, a lyrical, antibourgeois confession that addresses certain dilemmas of the intellectual after World War I.[16] Leiris's work is also a sort of justification for Sartre's own penchant for self-analysis—an activity that he otherwise spoke of with disdain.[17]

While Sartre may have manifested, at least in passing, the desire to be a poet, it is more his relationship to literature in general that is reminiscent of Leiris's attitude toward poetry. In *Les Mots,* Sartre writes of his early fascination with literature: "for a long time I considered the work of art as a metaphysical event whose birth interested the universe . . . I declared myself the licenced rescuer of the masses in order to gain my own salvation on the sly."[18] Leiris's remarks in the early 1930s, when he was writing (also nostalgically) of his surrealist days as a poet, are not unrelated: "The poet appeared to me like a predestined being, a sort of demiurge whose task was to effectuate the vast operation of the universe's mental transutation. . . .[19] Using religious terminology, both writers look wistfully back to an earlier pe-

15. Sartre, *Les Carnets de la drôle de guerre, Novembre 1939–Mars 1940* (Paris: Gallimard, 1983), 175.

16. Sartre's Presentation to the first issue of *Les Temps modernes* speaks indirectly of Leiris in a veiled reference that is both complimentary and critical: "After the other war [World War I] . . . the best writers, the purest, confessed publicly what could humiliate them the most and showed themselves to be satisfied when they had attracted bourgeois reprobation: they had produced a writing that, through its consequences, somewhat resembled an act." *Les Temps modernes* 1 (Oct. 1945): 2–3. Roland Simon has also pointed out certain connections between "De la littérature . . . " and Sartre's Presentation. See Roland-H. Simon, *Orphée médusé: Autobiographies de Michel Leiris* (Lausanne: L'Age d'homme, 1984), 114–15. Interestingly enough, Leiris is not so complimentary of *Les Mots* and prefers, "even literally," *L'Etre et le néant.* See: Madeleine Gobeil, "Interview with Michel Leiris," *SubStance* 11–12 (1975): 56–57. (The Gobeil interview appears in English in *SubStance.*)

17. Jean-Paul Sartre, *Les Carnets de la drôle de guerre,* 175. "I hated intimate notebooks and thought that man is not made for looking at himself. . . . I haven't changed. It's just that it seems one can, in certain important circumstances, and when one is changing one's life, like the serpent that sheds its skin, look at that dead skin . . . and take stock." For Sartre, Leiris's confession is intimately linked to (and justified by) the events of war (both World Wars).

18. Jean-Paul Sartre, *Les Mots* (Paris: Gallimard, 1964), 151, 153.

19. *L'Age d'homme,* (Paris: Gallimard, 1946, rpt. 1966), 216. In *Biffures,* 237, Leiris explains that he is now "quite far from the period when I saw in the act of writing something sacred."

riod of their lives when they believed literature, through the writer's self-sacrifice,[20] could save author and readers from the sin of unjustified existence. To both, autobiography is the place of lamenting literature's inadequacies or for recalling one's (lost?) illusions about it. But whereas Sartre eventually (if reluctantly) becomes resigned to the idea that literature can never stir itself into an act of sociopolitical import, Leiris's autobiographical works continue to believe in, and argue for, a commitment to poetic language that would invest the writer in his writing while necessarily remaining socially responsive. Ultimately, instead of using autobiography as a rejection of literature (as Sartre does with *Les Mots*), Leiris formally brings literature's "highest form"—poetry—into the last volume of his autobiography.

Because most of the aforementioned connections between Leiris's and Sartre's texts concern positions that Leiris had already taken before meeting or reading Sartre in the early 1940s, it is safe to say that their association did not consist of a simple, unidirectional influence, whether good or bad, of Sartre on Leiris. What is somewhat more difficult to ascertain is the nature of Leiris's existentialism. The vocabulary of the 1946 endnotes and presentation to *L'Age d'homme* ("De la littérature considérée comme une tauromachie"), and of *Biffures*, does have an existentialist ring.[21]

In "De la littérature . . ." Leiris values authenticity and "engagement," and he emphasizes the writer's responsibility to communicate with his readers. His existential anguish and feelings of guilt are consistent with Sartre's own in the early postwar years. But most importantly, Leiris stresses that his goal in *L'Age d'homme* was to make literature an *act*.[22] Leiris establishes a distance, however, between an existentialist literary act and the kind of act he was purporting to accomplish in *L'Age d'homme:* "It was less a matter of what is commonly called "committed literature" than a literature in which I tried

20. See: *Les Mots*, 151–52: "I mistook literature for prayer and made a human sacrifice. . . . I offered myself as an expiatory victim"; and *L'Age d'homme*, 216: "The poet also appeared to me—necessarily—as a damned soul, doomed for all eternity to an unhappy solitude. . . ."

21. In the notes to *L'Age d'homme* (251), Leiris moves away from his surrealist perspective of 1935, when he described his problem in terms of a castration complex, to his 1946 (existentialist) position in which the problem becomes: "the fear that I have of committing myself [m'engager], of assuming my responsibilities. . . ."

22. Roland Simon points out that in *Biffures*, Leiris uses Sartre's concept of "le regard d'autrui" (from *L'Etre et le néant*) to analyze his protective façades. See: *Orphée médusé*, 153.

to commit myself totally" (13). The explanation would appear to stand an existential goal of social commitment on its head. Whereas Leiris's self-portrait sought to transform its author, "waiting for it to modify me" (13), as he says, Sartre proclaims in the Presentation to *Les Temps modernes*: ". . . our intention is to work on producing certain changes in the society that surrounds us" (7). On the one hand, literature is the active agent to which the writer submits, whereas on the other, it is a tool for the social transformation (of others). Nevertheless, the postwar Leiris, editor at *Les Temps modernes*, can propose, however hesitatingly, that his earlier self-portrait is an act (involving risk and an esthetic rigor) that can be compared to the bullfighter's—after all, Sartre's Presentation states that one *cannot avoid action* (7). And *Biffures* continues to pursue the literary act as well, but it will be based on a thematics of rupture and without any claim to a lethal risk.

What becomes clear in reading Leiris, however, is that the seriousness of his existentialist position is jostled by his personal version of commitment and by a playful doubling. In "De la littérature . . . ," Leiris stresses more the *metaphorical* nature of the comparison between bullfighting and literature than its reality. In his 1966 interview with Madeleine Gobeil, Leiris eagerly points out the ironic doubling of his title, "De la littérature considérée comme une tauromachie" without, however, forsaking his initial idea of the author's "engagement" in literature:

> I am anxious to clarify the question of the "bullfighter" in what I have called "Of Literature Considered as a Tauromachy." . . . if I chose this title, it was for irony. . . . I reappropriated Thomas de Quincey's title: "Of Assassination Considered as one of the Fine Arts," which had been taken up again by Cocteau before *L'Age d'homme:* "Of Fine Arts Considered as an Assassination;" I took this title to show that literature is not a tauromachy; I was being ironic. We should try to make literature such that it would commit the author as much as the bullfighter . . . but I do not maintain it is so. . . . I have a conception of 'commitment' which differs from that of Sartre. I would like a 'commitment' which, of itself, rather than through its political consequences, is as dangerous as that of the bullfighter facing the bull. I mean a commitment which can lead some to suicide . . . some to madness. . . . [49][23]

23. This statement also raises interesting issues concerning the question of intentions in Leiris's work. See my article: "Getting into the (Speech) Act: Autobiography as Theory and Performance," *SubStance* 52 (1987): 39.

Coupled, then, with Leiris's deadly serious, quasi-existentialist reading of his work's merits and insufficiencies is an intertextual humor that challenges his own assertions about literature. And while at the end of volume 3, Leiris still maintains that "a poet cannot turn away from the fate of his neighbor" (*Fibrilles*, 266), he contests the more Sartrean principles among his autobiographical guidelines when he exclaims in almost comical exasperation: "Communication, authenticity, such words are decaying planks!" (*Fibrilles*, 286). These firm principles (dear to Sartre) are deemed too nebulous or too simplistic to be effective for Leiris's doubled-edged writing. Whereas both writers thematize the difficulty of distinguishing between (false) gestures and (authentic) acts, Leiris tends to play upon the possibilities of the ambivalence, while Sartre deplores it.

To say this, however, is not to rule out the importance of Sartre's thought for Leiris, particularly during the war when he was beginning *La Règle du jeu*. For if *Biffures* is oriented around the poetic movements of "bifurs," that is, bifurcations or "the glidings of thought happening at the moment of a break . . . swirls, wrinkles, froth or other alterations in the surface . . . of language . . ." (280), it *also* contains a critical movement: "biffures," that is, erasures or "successive eliminations of illusory values" (284). The "biffures" serve to criticize—and socialize—the potentially solipsistic elucubrations of the autobiographer who is busy linking and arranging his index cards recounting the past. Sartre's theories of "engagement" remind Leiris of what he already knew: that his research into the writing of the self ("s'engageant dans la littérature") desperately needs its readership. The famous ". . . Reusement!" episode at the beginning of *Biffures*, when the little boy Michel learns that the word is "heureusement" and not "reusement," dramatizes Leiris's recognition that language is not just his private possession, but rather the "arachnean web of [one's] rapport with others . . ." (10). The anecdote provides a framework for Leiris's entire autobiographical enterprise. However troublesome Leiris might at times feel this social responsibility in language, it is also an *integral* part of the poet-autobiographer's work rather than a temporary supplement, because it helps to bring the writer out of an unbearable solitude synonymous with death: "facing the *it* or the *they* of objects having become menacing . . . only the *I* is left in its alveole. But what is an *I*— an *I* alone and isolated—without a *you*, without a *we*, without a *he* gravitating around him . . .?" (*Biffures*, 79). Whether in *Biffures* in the

1940s or *Langage tangage* in the 1980s, Leiris's work maintains the tension between the seductions of language and its social functions.

LEIRIS AND THE NEW NOVEL

Leiris's name is not often associated with those of the New Novelists, although many of their ideas about literature are similar and are consonant with a modern (post-Sartrean) understanding of the subject's position in language. In both cases, language is not in a simple mimetic relationship to an external reality; the text shapes/creates its object rather than imitating a pre-extant one and the lines between fiction and a "true account" (of a story, of a past) are blurred. Language is not so much a tool for communication as a generator of meanings that exceed the particular speaker/writer. As Leiris recognizes: "[language] is this instrument that one imagines one is maneuvering, whereas in fact very often it is language that is maneuvering you . . ." (*Langage tangage,* 146). And Claude Simons' use of Lévi-Strauss's term "bricolage" to designate the novelist's concrete activity is particularly well suited to describe Leiris's autobiographical "bif(f)ur(e)s" as he works with his index cards:

> Indeed, I do not know a term that brings out better the completely crafted, empirical character of this labor which consists of assembling and organizing . . . all these components [that] must *answer each other in echos* in the vast system called a novel. It is done through successive gropings: there are elements that one must plane or file . . . add . . . reject . . . "fabricate". . . . And the most fascinating . . . is that the purely formal necessities, far from constituting constraints or obstacles, prove to be eminently *productive. . . .*[24]

Although in Leiris's case, the writer is no doubt less sanguine about the actual success of the move from formal game to personal discovery, the methodological procedures of the New Novelist and the autobiographer are quite similar. In addition, Leiris and the New Novelists recreate the literary genres they are working in by discarding or challenging various conventions: they distrust traditional, closed, linear

---

24. Claude Simon, "La Fiction mot à mot," in *Nouveau Roman: hier, aujourd'hui,* ed. Jean Ricardou and Françoise von Rossum-Guyon (Paris: Union Générale d'Editions, 1972), vol. 2, 96–97. One can also associate Leiris's methods with those of Raymond Roussel.

structures, as well as simple forms of causality. In their writings, the text tends to display its own genesis and is self-representational, operating its own critique from within.

Leiris's choice of autobiography, rather than "pure fiction," does, of course, distinguish his work considerably from the New Novel. He fully acknowledges his personal investment in the writing and does not eschew the possibility of a referential link with an "outside" of literature. And although the writers associated with the New Novel are very different from one another, moral responsibility and guilt do not tend to color their fictional landscapes—whereas Sartre's and Leiris's works thematize them.[25] In a 1986 interview, Robbe-Grillet exclaims that neither he nor his characters ever feel moral responsibility or guilt.[26] Finally, the flurry of New Novelists's autobiographies in the past ten years fits the more traditional urge of the well established writer than it does Leiris's endeavor to transform himself via writing.

In his interview with Gobeil, Leiris distances himself from Robbe-Grillet:

> I'm quite fond of Robbe-Grillet, but reproach him with his theoretical side and with stretching his own theories. In his book *Dans le labyrinthe*, he begins with an extremely serious note in which he warns the reader not to imagine anything whatever beyond what is presented. But, manifestly, everything that is presented is designed to invoke this beyond in order for the reader to see something other than what is related. Frankly, this irritates me a bit. [57]

Leiris takes issue with Robbe-Grillet's offhand rejection of his text's representational effects (and with his manipulation of the reader), and would no doubt have been closer to Michel Butor and Nathalie Sarraute in the early '70s, when the latter were taken to task by Robbe-Grillet, Jean Ricardou and their followers, for intimating a rapport in their fiction with an extratext.[27]

Michel Butor is the New Novelist with whom Leiris has felt the greatest kinship. Their mutual appreciation in the 1950s is marked by

25. Butor's *La Modification* is, of course, a notable exception.
26. Alain Robbe-Grillet, "The Art of Fiction XCI," *Paris Review* 99 (Spring, 1986), 49.
27. See the discussions of Sarraute's and Butor's work in *Nouveau Roman: Hier, aujourd'hui*, vol. 2, 41-57 and 279–95. Robbe-Grillet will considerably soften his stance on the text's total self-enclosure in his own autobiography, *Le Miroir qui revient* (Paris: Editions de Minuit, 1985).

Leiris's article on Butor's novel, *La Modification*,[28] and by Butor's article on *L'Age d'homme* and the first two volumes of *La Règle du jeu*. In Butor's article, the New Novelist situates Leiris's autobiography where he would probably also place the New Novel: equidistant from "art for art's sake" and from a "a committed literature." His characterization of *La Règle du jeu* as "a dialectical autobiography," aptly brings into play the notion of a dialogue between the Leiris of the past and the writing "I" of the present, while it also intimates the indispensable dialogue between the autobiographer and his readers. Not only are these interlocutors virtual participants in autobiography, notes Butor, they are an active part of Leiris's work. In *Biffures*, Leiris actually quotes others' negative criticisms of the chapter "Dimanche" that he had already published in *Les Temps modernes*. Butor stresses that the reader/critic of Leiris's autobiography becomes an active partner in the dialogue and Butor maintains that the reader shares in the responsibility for the autobiographer's successes and failures.

This active involvement of the reader is certainly part of what attracts Leiris to *La Modification*. With a playful mimicry, Leiris begins his article by using the "you" that Butor so handily used in his novel to indicate both the internal dialogue of his character and the inclusion of the readers who feel they too are being implicated in the character's thoughts. And for the author of "Le Sacré dans la vie quotidienne," the way Butor links the commonplace plot of the novel to cultural, mythical associations of European civilization cannot fail to attract. As is the case in many New Novels, myth and tragedy are integral to Leiris's autobiography, but he is particularly sensitive to Butor's mythic reworking of the commonplace, and sees in it the possibility for any reader to identify with the mythic:

> [it's] as if the menacing use of the formal *you* [vous] were an effective incitement for you too to become aware and to enter into action in such a way that the story of this Parisian bourgeois—whom about twenty hours of train ride have enlightened about his true desires—becomes . . . an equivalent of our own story and, in its strictly photographic modernity, the myth through which the mediocrity of your existence takes on the elevated appearance of a destiny. [*Brisées*, 235]

28. "Le Réalisme mythologique de Michel Butor," in *Brisées* (Paris: Mercure de France, 1966), 215-38. Originally published in *Critique* 129 (1958).

Leiris is attracted to *La Modification*'s autobiographical allure—"this book which for its supposed author [the main character], is a fragment of autobiography" (*Brisées*, 235). He also stresses the novel's authenticity: even if it is fiction, it offers a quest for both supposed author and real author to learn who they are. In addition, the formal "you" (vous) implicitly addressing the reader implicates the latter in the quest. The New Novel often presents itself as a search for, and questioning of, personal identity. In Butor's case, the solution proposed—to write about the search—is one that is in keeping with the way Leiris conceives of his own autobiographical enterprise. The second-person novel, akin to the first-person autobiographical form, still retains the belief in some sort of rapport between the self and the world.[29] Contrary to certain later developments in poststructural theories of language, Butor's work—and in fact most New Novels (despite what Robbe-Grillet has at times said)—do not do away with some notion of subjective agency in language. Leiris's continued use of the autobiographical "I" in dialogue with itself acknowledges agency without reifying the "self."

The "modification" brought about in the life of Butor's character is no doubt reminiscent of Leiris's call to "changer la vie" (and himself in the process). For both, the transformation occurs in a game of "qui-perd-gagne" [loser wins] which one never quite controls.[30] Interestingly enough, Sartre also uses the expression "qui perd gagne" at the end of *Les Mots* in describing his unwillingness to give up faith in literature's power: "I sometimes wonder if I don't play the game of "loser wins" and strive to trample my past hopes in order that everything be returned to me a hundredfold" (213). Whereas Sartre reproaches himself with this game, as a form of "bad faith," Butor and Leiris conceive of it as a sometimes bittersweet, yet fortuitous transformation that literature can make happen, beyond the realm of clear-cut intentions.[31]

---

29. Robbe-Grillet dissociates *his* group from such a goal in fiction: "[Butor] always tries to find a possible understanding ["un accord"] between the "I" and the world, whereas for us that scarcely has any meaning any more." See: *Nouveau Roman: hier, aujourd'hui*, vol. 2, 283.

30. This is the expression that Leiris uses in his article (*Brisées*, 238), to describe the end of Butor's novel.

31. In addition to the formal links between Leiris's autobiography and Butor's fiction, there are others, of a purely anecdotal nature, that must have appeared quite uncanny to Leiris when he first read the novel in 1957. He reads of Butor's ageing bourgeois male contemplating his mediocre life, and debating about whether or not to

Although Leiris never mentions them, novels like *Entre la Vie et la mort* and *Les Fruits d'or* by Nathalie Sarraute effectively stage the drama of literary creation and reception, in such a way that, like the autobiographer of *La Règle du jeu*, the novelist is continually (re)enacting the difficulties and pleasures of her own literary production. In *L'Ere du soupçon*, her collection of theoretical essays on the novel, Sarraute defends her own literary experimentation (in contrast to the already established existentialist novel) by positing a male writer (a thinly disguised self-portrait) who bears an uncanny resemblance to Leiris in his autobiographical quest. Sarraute describes her unknown writer as a solitary "unhappy diehard," ["un malheureux obstiné"] who is obsessed with certain internal movements (detected in his childhood) that he thinks all people bear inside of them. Like the Leiris of *Biffures* who turns to autobiography (and away from the large scale events of the war), Sarraute's hypothetical writer is "turned in on himself, steeping in the protective liquid of his tightly closed little jar. . . ."[32] What this ill-adapted man has to give derives from his inspection of minute reactions in himself—what Sarraute calls "tropisms"—and that he hopes to show exist in everyone. The tropism's double movement of attraction and repulsion toward a stimulant (object, person, word . . .) resembles the double movement in Leiris's bif(f)ur(e)s: a writing that presents and criticizes ["une écriture qui énonce et dénonce"],[33] never settling definitively on one meaning, but always oscillating between positions (the interval where we, as readers, precariously reside).

In *Fourbis*, Leiris too defends this introspection that looks like a mania if viewed from the perspective of large scale Actions and Events (the kind that interest Sartre and de Beauvoir). Leiris hesitantly asks:

> Isn't it, nonetheless, one of the most natural goals of literary activity . . . to forge, with lived experience as the base and with language as the tool, certain attempts at truth that some will accept as their own and which, through the very act of this sharing, will cease to be lonely chimeras or vain appearances? [65]

---

leave his wife for another woman, at a time when he, Leiris, is recovering from an attempted suicide in part due to a similar sort of personal predicament. Butor's ending—with his character Léon Delmont deciding to write about his decision—must have seemed to Leiris like an appeal to write about his own dilemma and its outcome. Which is what he does in *Fibrilles* . . .

32. Nathalie Sarraute, *L'Ere du soupçon* (Paris: Gallimard, 1956), 102, 103.
33. I have borrowed Roland Simon's description here (*Orphée médusé*, 121).

Sarraute's indirect justification of herself could just as well apply to Leiris (in the form of the "loser wins" game):

> . . . it can happen that individuals who are isolated, ill adapted, solitary, morbidly attached to their childhood and turned in upon themselves, cultivating a more or less conscious taste for a certain form of failure, succeed, by abandoning themselves to an apparently useless passion, in pulling out and bringing to light a small fragment of an as yet unknown reality. [*L'Ere du soupçon*, 182]

The dialogues between writer and reader, or its internal versions within one individual, are essential to both Sarraute's and Leiris's projects. Having lived and written in the margins of existentialism,[34] Sarraute and Leiris justify their novels and autobiography respectively against the backdrop of the action, event-oriented literature that de Beauvoir and Sartre were advocating. Sarraute's tropism is another variation of the "malaise," when one loses one's footing. Like Leiris's bif(f)ur(e)s, the daily commonplace non-event becomes the site of intense drama and questioning. Ultimately, the New Novelist and the autobiographer are concerned with gleaning from their own experience in language something that will reveal to themselves and to others a better understanding of their human condition and their life. This literary act does not fit Sartre's descriptions, but the latter no doubt helped to erect action as a literary value with which Leiris and the New Novelists had to contend. For the (post)modern writer like Leiris, the "loser wins" game encompasses both a literary guile (akin to trickery as it was for Sartre), and a radical, dizzying chance to write with unforeseen effects.

34. Sarraute also published in *Les Temps modernes* in the late 1940s and Sartre wrote a preface for her first full-fledged novel, *Portrait d'un inconnu* (Paris: Robert Marin, 1948).

MICHÈLE RICHMAN

Leiris's *L'Age d'homme:* Politics and the Sacred in Everyday Ethnography

Readers of *L'Afrique fantôme* will recall the scene: following seventy pages detailing the minutiae of the expedition's first five months, the entry for 31 August 1931 marks a welcome highpoint. In the village of Nkourala, Leiris and his colleagues observe a sacrificial offering which involves the use of a fetish: "C'est une masse informe qui, lorsque les quatre hommes, avec précaution, l'ont sorti de son antre, se révèle, être un sac de toile grossière et rapiécée, couvert d'une sorte de bitume qui est de sang coagulé, bourré à l'intérieur de choses qu'on devine poussiéreuses et hétéroclites, muni à un bout d'une protubérance . . . et clochette à l'autre[1] [It is an amorphous mass which, as the four men lift it with great care from its niche, turns out to be a sack of coarse, patched canvas, covered with a sort of pitch made of congealed blood, stuffed with what one guesses to be an assortment of dusty things, with a protuberance at one end and a small bell at the other]. The description stops there, as could have Leiris's narrative. But, unexpectedly, given the author's lamented inability to "engage" in the scene he is witnessing and recording, Leiris provides the following commentary:

> Grand émoi religieux: objet sale, simple, élémentaire dont l'abjection est une terrible force parce qu'y est condensé l'absolu de ces hommes et qu'ils y ont imprimé leur propre force, comme dans la petite boulette de terre qu'un enfant roule entre ses doigts quand il joue avec la boue." [*AF*, 78]

1. Michel Leiris, *L'Afrique fantôme* (Paris: Editions Gallimard [1934] 1981), 78. References in text are designated by *AF*. Translations are my own.

YFS 81, *On Leiris,* ed. Blanchard, © 1992 by Yale University.

Great religious effusion brought by this simple, dirty object whose abjection is a fantastic force because men have condensed into it their own sense of the absolute, and that they have imprinted their own power in it, as in the little ball of earth a child rolls between his fingers when playing with clay.

Surprise? Leiris, self-confessedly impotent observer, congenitally condemned to the detachment awarded the ethnographer, nonetheless here experiences one of those rare moments of empathic identification and total grasp of the situation he equates with a poetic *saisie*. Why this exceptional adhesion in relatively unexceptional circumstances? The bloodletting is not accompanied by external inducements such as music, trance, or possession, aside from the drinking of the intoxicant *dolo* among the natives, to whom it imparts "une noblesse d'allure et laquelle n'atteignent presque jamais les musulmans" (*AF*, 78) [an air of nobility rarely attained by Muslims]. Less than two weeks later, Leiris concludes an "adventure" of dubious moral standards on the part of aggressive ethnographers in quest of another fetish. Faced with a general paralysis among the indigenous population fearful of the fetish's power, Griaule and Leiris themselves take it, wrap the sacred object and leave "comme des voleurs, cependant que le chef affolé s'enfuit et, à quelque distance, fait rentrer dans une case sa femme et ses enfants en les frappant à grands coups de baton" (*AF*, 82) [like thieves, while the panic-stricken chief flees at a safe distance, forces his wife and children into a hut while flogging them with a stick]. Unwrapping the reward for their "affreux chantage" [despicable extortion] they find an enormous mask of a vaguely animal-like form, "malheureusement détérioré, mais entièrement recouvert d'une croûte de sang coagulé qui lui confère la majesté que le sang confère à toutes choses . . . " (*AF*, 83) [unfortunately deteriorated, but entirely covered with a layer of coagulated blood which confers upon it the majesty which blood imparts to all things . . .]. Later on, we find the description of a *tam-tam*, where music induces a trance in some, while others "feign" a semblance of epilepsy, and yet others indulge in erotic amusements: "Noblesse extrême de la débauche, de la magie et du charlatanisme. Tout ceci est religieux, et je suis décidément un homme religieux . . . " (*AF*, 86) [The extreme dignity of debauchery, of magic and of charlatanism. All this is religious and I am decidedly a religious man].

These brief, intermittent spurts of intense participation with the object of study can be contrasted with the frequent bouts of ennui which afflict the author during the first phase of the expedition, when the vast African continent and its inhabitants appear as so many shadows of their former selves. But Leiris is also haunted by the formidable ghosts of his own past, and the fear that he will never penetrate anything in depth, "Ne tenir que des bribes d'un tas de choses me met en rage" (AF, 105) [The inability to grasp no more than bits and pieces infuriates me]. Equally disturbing is that the paralysis brought on by his own demons leads to outbursts of compensatory aggression, not unlike the case of the chief cited above.

With the approach of the Abyssinian border, Part 1 closes with a sense of anticipation that the fantasies which prompted Leiris to join the group may finally be realized: "Combien de kilomètres a-t-il fallu que nous fassions pour nous sentir enfin au seuil de l'exotisme!" (AF, 226) [How many kilometers were needed to bring us to the threshold of exoticism?]. Indeed, only after Leiris arrives in Abyssinia does the pace of the narrative quicken and the observations of indigenous practices intensify. Finally, at Gondar, Leiris seems to fulfill the goals of the official mission as well as overcome his personal inhibitions by immersing himself in the experience of the *zar* or spirits of possession. Two experiences are particularly noteworthy: one follows a sacrifice where the author's head has been anointed with butter in the traditional fashion: "Resté sur la banquette je me sens très séparé, très saint, très élu. Je pense à ma première communion: si elle avait été aussi grave que cela, peut-être serais-je resté croyant; mais la vraie religion ne commence qu'avec le sang" (AF, 443) [Alone on the bench I feel very separate, very saintly, even chosen. I remember my first communion, if it had been as solemn, perhaps I would have remained a believer; but true religion begins with blood]. Then, trying to explain a surge of extraordinary appetite and his ability to satisfy it, he remarks, "Il faut vraiment que ce soit le zar qui mange, non le "cheval," car je ne me serais jamais soupçonné une telle capacité" (AF, 443) [Undoubtedly, it must be the zar eating, not the 'horse,' for I would never have suspected myself capable of such an appetite].

Although relations with the people of Gondar undergo the usual vicissitudes, Leiris's interest in their rituals is sustained throughout most of his stay. When his passions flag, it is often due to the resurgence of repressed effects of a civilization which colors everything with a moral judgment rather than a magical aura, or the return of the demons he shares with other victims of a "stupid" bourgeois-Catholic upbringing. Despite such ongoing turmoil, reflections like this one appear: "Et jamais je n'avais senti à quel point je suis religieux, mais d'une religion où il est nécessaire qu'on me fasse voir le dieu . . . "[2] (*AF*, 374) [Never had I realized to what extent I am religious, but of a religion where it is necessary to show me the god . . .]. Indeed, what fascinates Leiris in the rituals he observes if not the possibility of an experience of the sacred devoid of any reference to a godhead or institutionalized religion? Moreover, is it not possible to trace the attraction exerted by Leiris's text to precisely his ambivalence between the quest for *moments parfaits* and the frustration of not being able to overcome a paralyzing void within?

The question prompting this essay, then, is what becomes of the "religious" sentiment or the issues raised by the examples of the sacred in other cultures in Leiris's subsequent writings. Earlier critical works addressing the same questions tend to emphasize a break with the sanguinary, dramatic rituals of *L'Afrique fantôme* in order to emphasize an attenuated, i.e., personalized version of the sacred, with its final displacement by *le merveilleux* in *Frêle bruit*.[3] The recreation of such a trajectory is facilitated in one instance by skipping over *l'Age d'homme* (which Leiris was outlining at the same time as *L'Afrique fantôme*) in order to focus exclusively on the 1938 address to the *Collège de sociologie*, "Le Sacré dans la vie quotidienne."[4] Jamin duly notes the modifications to the Durkheimian model it presents: rather than the eminently social and collective phenomenon celebrated in the *Elementary Forms of Religious Life*, Leiris's sacred appears to be individualized (if not entirely individual), the outcome of childhood experiences and games shared with friends and siblings. Using Bataille's dramatic version as foil, Jamin contrasts the notion of *dépense*, where expenditure, loss, sacrifice, eroticism, and violence form the basis for sacred communication, with Leiris's "left" sacred, in the sense of "gauche," awkward or uncomfortable. In Jamin's presentation, Leiris does not actively transgress the rules of conduct and bourgeois respectability so much as he trips over the subtle lines of acceptability. The oft-maligned physical timidity and weaknesses are transmuted into agents of genteel subversion. His hero is a maternal uncle *déclassé*

2. Marcel Moré interprets most references to religion and this one in particular as a sign that Leiris was indeed seeking a religious revelation in the traditional sense. See his "L'Afrique fantôme" in *L'Ire des vents* 3–4 (1981), 191–99.

3. See Paul Chaton de Brancion, "La Chouette de Minerve: Du sacré au merveilleux chez le littérateur Michel Leiris, *Revue Romane* v. 18 (1983), 45–60.

4. See Jean Jamin, "Quand le sacré devint gauche," *L'Ire des vents* 4 (1981), 98–118.

by joining the circus, rather than revolutionaries who seek to abolish classes altogether. Like Proust and his *faux pas*, Leiris seems to stumble onto his epiphanies when least expected. His only "method," is a willingness to stray from the established path. Self-knowledge begins with the "look" inflicted by others who first point out the *maladresses* subsequently metamorphosed by the poet into signs of election. Firmly anchored in a quotidian punctuated by ephemeral breakthroughs, this version of the sacred rapidly shifts focus onto the "open sesame" power of language, albeit through a poetics of linguistic perversions, deviations and *demi-entendres.*

However endearing, this portrait of the artist as young clod bypasses the more complex representation of the sacred found in *L'Age d'homme.* By isolating Leiris's version from the violently disruptive and transgressive forces associated with the traditional anthropological sense of the "left" sacred, its crucial proximity to death has been effectively kept at bay. Yet "tears of eros" (Bataille) are shed throughout Leiris's work as a sort of ritual ablution of unconsummated sexuality, and the exaltation associated with eroticism is experienced as an uncontrolled *chavirement* or unsettling of the illusory stability of bourgeois order. The terror evoked by the loved one is so extreme that the usually garrulous author finds himself mute. Most importantly, the bullfight functions as the standard by which other simulated and less admired rituals of *mise à mort* are gauged. Early on, Leiris expresses as much concern for the manner with which death is met as with the terror elicited by the phenomenon itself. The standard Master/Slave dialectic is disrupted by his identification with the victim who nonetheless ultimately triumphs. In his favorite mythological pantheon, Judith and Lucretia transform their horrific situations into parables of strength, offering dramas in which the victim/executioner relationship is played out with unexpected heroism. The question of how death is met challenges the bourgeois mediocrity feared by the young Leiris, who contrasts the violent ending of monsters and *maudits* appropriate to their exceptional natures with the tranquility of family members expiring in their domestic beds.

Another revealing example of how the sacred is introduced includes memories of a 1927 trip to Greece. On Mount Olympus, he cannot resist making a "libation of a certain order" to the temple of Zeus; the intimate offering flows on the tender grey stone: "J'avais nettement l'idée—pas littéraire du tout, mais vraiment spontanée—qu'il s'agissait d'un sacrifice, avec tout ce que ce mot 'sacrifice' comporte de mystique et de grisant" [I had the distinct sense—not at all literary, but truly spontaneous—that I had offered a *sacrifice*, with all that this word implies of the mystical and the intoxicating].[5]

The encounter of traditionally antithetical sensations is replicated most intensely in the erotic experience or, more accurately, in any of those adventures relating to sexuality where fear and terror accompany excitement and desire. Leiris then traces the association to his earliest childhood when he and his friends invented ritual ceremonies in the course of which they terrorized his young niece "en même temps que nous faisions obscurément coïncider l'érotisme et la peur . . . " (*AH*, 63) [at the same time that we obscurely combined eroticism and fear . . . *MH*, 54]. Later on, the configuration of sentiments evoked will be most accurately rendered by the bullfight analogy which continues to be more "real" in its sacrifice than any religious offering "parce que le sacrificateur y est constamment menacé de la mort, et d'un coup matériel—enchassé dans les cornes—au lieu de la mort magique, c'est-à-dire fictive, à laquelle s'expose quiconque entre en contact trop abrupt avec le surnaturel" (*AH*, 75) [because here the sacrificer is constantly threatened with death, and with a bodily catastrophe—being caught on the horns—instead of the magical, i.e., fictional disaster which threatens anyone entering into too abrupt a contact with the supernatural *MH*, 64].

The parallels with the sexual act are underscored, given the unusual combination of both "union" and "combat" in the bullfight, "ainsi qu'il en est de l'amour et des cérémonies sacrificielles, sans lesquelles il y a contact étroit avec la victime . . . " (*AH*, 77 [as there is in love and in sacrificial ceremonies, in which there is close contact with the victim . . . *MH*, 65]. Indeed, the persistent power of the bullfight resides in its "allure" of a religious ceremony where, unlike those of modern religion which allow only for a symbolic mode of sacrifice, the stakes are the highest possible for both man and animal. Eschewing dramaturgical metaphors, Leiris thus proclaims "L'essentiel n'est donc pas le spectacle, mais l'élément sacrificiel, gestes stricts accomplis à deux doigts de la mort pour donner la mort" (*AH*, 81) [It is therefore not the spectacle that is essential but the sacrifice, the pre-

5. Michel Leiris, *L'Age d'homme* (Paris: Editions Gallimard, 1946), 62. Henceforth, all references in text indicated by *AH*. *Manhood*. Trans. Richard Howard (Great Britain: Jonathan Cape Ltd., 1968), 53. References in text indicated by *MH*.

cise gestures performed on the brink of death and in order to inflict death *MH*, 69].

Early sensations reminiscent of the sacred are traced to Leiris's Catholic background. He recounts the childhood impact of the story of the vestal virgin condemned to live entombment for having allowed the sacred fire to burn out. The passages from *L'Afrique fantôme* cited above repudiating the nefarious effects of a Catholic upbringing are repeated here, albeit with less vehemence. Instead, the issue is broached with a dose of levity, when the author describes how the fervor surrounding his first communion dissipates at the same rate as the holy wafer dissolves!

Leiris is closest to the sensibility of his friend Bataille—at the origin of this book—when he perceives the powerful emotions elicited by any rapprochement with death as providing the affective substrata of the erotic experience. Although Leiris lacks the energetic excess Bataille vaunted, his descriptions of the loss of footing experienced when lovers are propelled into a vertiginous "retour au chaos," (*AH*, 93) [return to chaos" *MH*, 80] are reminiscent of scenes in Bataille's *Histoire de l'oeil* (1929). As Bataille often insisted, lovemaking resembles a fit or, as Leiris echoes, a spasm "dont on n'a jamais à proprement parler conscience, à cause de toutes les facultés qu'il implique . . . dans l'aventure sexuelle comme dans la mort le point culminant de cette crise s'accompagne d'une perte de conscience, au moins partielle dans le premier cas . . . " (*AH*, 193) [of which one is never conscious strictly speaking, because of the collapse of all the faculties which it implies . . . in the sexual involvement as in death the climax is accompanied by a loss of consciousness, at least partial in the former case *MH*, 80].

But whereas Bataille always strained a rhetorical muscle to maintain his discourse at the level of death Leiris explores the downside of the *jouissance* cycle as well. Fearful that his love is diminishing, he recounts scratching his entire body with scissors "avec une sorte d'enragée et voluptueuse application" (*AH*, 101) [with a kind of furious and voluptuous determination *MH*, 87]. The powerful scene compares with nothing less than the photo of Chinese torture which holds a privileged place within Bataillian iconography. Leiris's illustration of the encounter of opposites in a sacred violence erupting within daily life introduces a chapter where images of wounds, painful penetration, and mutilation are associated with sacrificial scarification and a pathological reaction to female genitals. Scenes of arrows shooting into the eye of a family servant who claims he has put it out, or the experience of putting a finger into moistened bread all partake of an "indescribable horror." Moreover, the "profound" significance of the pierced eye is related to a tendency to regard the female organ ["as a wound' [*MH*, 74]. Like all objects, persons, or experiences assembled under the category of the sacred, the female sex organ elicits ambivalent reactions. Leiris describes the tension underlying opposing sentiments in his essay on the sacred in everyday life as a mixture of "crainte et attachement, attirante et dangereuse, prestigieuse et rejetée . . . " [fear and attachment, that ambiguous attitude caused by the approach of something simultaneously attractive and dangerous, prestigious and outcast . . .]; in sum, the encounter of respect, desire and terror as well as dirt and repulsion.[6] When "holy terror" is lacking, Leiris replaces it with pity, in order to provoke "une sorte de déchirement moral au sein de la vie quotidienne, tentant de la changer un peu, grâce à ces affres répétées, en un 'radeau de la Méduse' où se lamentent et se dévorent une poignée d'affamés" (*AH*, 164] [a kind of moral laceration which I introduce into everyday life, trying to transform it somewhat by these repeated pangs into a 'Raft of the Medusa' on which a handful of starved survivors mourn and devour each other *MH*, 140]. The overriding sentiment is described as an exaltation of a particular order linked, especially in the realm of sexuality, to terror. If Leiris experiences difficulties of expression, they are caused by a mixture of terror and pity which simulates a tragedy without catharsis. Overwhelmed by the encounter of antithetical feelings—tenderness and anxiousness—the author remains suspended in a state of confusion, in "cette impression de pétrification et de membres cassés qui ne m'a jamais quitté et qui m'étreint toujours, dès que je suis en face de l'amour" (*AH*, 187] [that sense of paralysis and collapse which still overcomes me when I am in the presence of love *MH*, 158].

These flashes of sacred intensity, however anguishing, lend their special color to the otherwise bland daily life of a petty bourgeois Parisian intellectual. Certainly the harshest characterization within this familial drama is reserved for the narrator's older brother—"celui

6. Michel Leiris, "Le Secré dans la vie quotidienne," in *Le Collège de sociologie* (1937–39), ed. Denis Hollier (Paris: Editions Gallimard, 1979), 60. *The College of Sociology* (1937–39) trans. Betsy Wing. (Minnesota: The University of Minnesota Press, 1988), 24.

que je n'aime pas" [the one I do not love]. From Leiris's generally cour-
teous pen spews the devastating portrait of an archetypal bourgeois,
recriminated for his self-satisfied airs, for being "sentimental sans
passion, désiste sans mysticisme, bien pensant sans fanatisme" and
especially for exuding "son impression de complète sécurité . . . "
(*AH*, 125) [sentimental without passion, deistic without mysticism,
respectable without fanaticism, the impression he gives of complete
security *MH*, 108]. Despite his own alleged timidity and physical infir-
mities, Leiris breaks with the security of his milieu when he undertakes the voyage to Africa or the autobiographical excursion to the
limits of being played out according to the rules of the bullfight. The
fascination exerted by such vulnerable exposure is that it reveals
the limits as well as possibilities of "ruptures" with the milieu of
origin. For this reason we can begin to appreciate the ambivalence
expressed toward psychoanalysis, despite its possible analytical insights into the origins of the "intimate mythology" fabricated through
dreams, erotic fantasies, and literary precedents. Leiris explicitly rejects its therapeutic telos, "ma répugnance pour tout ce qui prétend
guérir les maux autres que ceux du corps . . . " (*AH*, 43)]my repug-
nance for anything claiming to cure ills other than those of the body
MH, 37] even though the extremes of internal distress compelled him
to undergo psychotherapy.

The explicit repudiation of the alleged psychoanalytic reduc-
tionism is related to the constellation of figures derived from classical
as well as biblical antiquity through which the author expresses some
of his most complicated emotional states. Describing his attachment
to the diptych of female figures, Judith and Lucretia, Leiris points out
that the particular mixture of sacred terror and pity they evoke is
tinged with a sense of remorse due to his own cowardice as well as
cruelty, which in turn prompt the "crainte superstitieuse d'un châtiment" (*AH*, 164) [the superstitious fear of punishment *MH*, 140]. But
because Leiris also envisages himself as victim, he is absolved of any
guilt. Thus, despite considerable floundering in the inexplicable "confusion" of terror and pity, he aggressively declares:

> Que les explorateurs modernes de l'inconscient parlent d'Oedipe, de
> castration, de culpabilité, de narcissisme, je ne crois pas que cela avance
> beaucoup quant à l'essentiel du problème (qui reste selon moi apparen-
> té au problème de la mort, à l'appréhension du néant et relève donc de la
> métaphysique). [*AH*, 165]

When modern investigators invoke the unconscious, refer to Oedipus, castration, guilt and narcissism, I do not think this advances us greatly as to the essentials of the problem (which remains, I believe, linked to the problem of death, to the apprehension of nothingness, and therefore concerns metaphysics). [*MH*, 141]

The crucial rapprochement between beauty and death or fear and beauty underlying the fascination for both female figures is illuminated by an anecdote. At the time that the author began to discover modern poetry (1920–21), one of his most violent scenes with his father was prompted by the latter's declaration that Apollinaire's poems, the following two lines in particular, were absurd and incomprehensible: "Cette femme était si belle / Qu'elle me faisait peur" (*AH*, 166) [That woman was so lovely / She terrified me *MH*, 141].

The incident is especially revealing since the apparent cause of misunderstanding between father and son is neither political nor obviously moral but aesthetic. One could argue that the continuity of modern sensibility with nineteenth-century precedents lies in the expanded appreciation of taste as subsuming ethics, moral sensibility, and even politics. In the case of Leiris, this tendency is corroborated by the fact that most references to the paternal household and its "education" focus on matters of taste to illustrate the basis for alienation, as evidenced in the description of the tableau of the "Lion amoureux," or the witheringly funny anecdote regarding a bronze "charmeuse de serpent" of which his father was particularly proud: "Ce qu'il y a de joli, c'est que bien qu'elle soit nue elle est quand même très chaste ... " (*AH*, 96) ['What's really lovely about the piece is that, although she's naked, she's very chaste all the same' *MH*, 83]. Because of his father's predilection for a "sensualité bébête" (*AH*, 96) [sentimental sexuality *MH*, 82], the author finds it impossible to imagine anything of an erotic nature between his parents.

In his quest for evasion Leiris experiments with the alternatives that have become the common legacy to succeeding generations of avant-garde artists and rebels from their predecessors in the previous century. Preeminent, of course, is love, now envisioned in terms antithetical to the domesticated sentimentality of bourgeois marriage and therefore as sacred, erotic, and an integral part of the general movement *hors de soi*. The contradiction inherent in trying to sustain over time such sensations is rediscovered by Leiris this way:

L'amour, seule possibilité de coïncidence entre le sujet et l'objet, seul moyen d'accéder au sacré que représente l'objet convoité dans la mesure où il nous est un monde extérieur et étrange—implique sa propre négation du fait que tenir le sacré c'est en même temps le profaner et finalement le détruire en le dépouillant peu à peu de son caractère d'étrangeté. Un amour durable, c'est un sacré qui met longtemps à s'épuiser. [AH, 191]

Love—the only possibility of a coincidence between subject and object, the only means of acceding to the sacred, as represented by the desired object in so far as it is exterior and alien to us—implies its own negation because to possess the sacred is at the same time to profane and finally to destroy it by gradually robbing it of its alien character. [MH, 162]

At this stage of his life, the author begins to turn toward poetry, viewed as a refuge or escape from the ravages of time eroding the love relationship as well as a reminder of his own mortality. Ironically, he is pushed toward a conventional bourgeois marriage against his "désirs réels" (AH, 197) [real inclinations MH, 167] for totally unexpected reasons. As his father lies dying, his parents exchange glances—their final embrace—and the author must acknowledge the power of constancy and its own force in the face of the Absolute.

Thus, in contrast with Bataille's uncompromising and subversive exhortations for an "expenditure without reserve," Leiris concedes his own attraction to the "pure" side of the sacred: "car pour arriver à une certaine intensité dans l'impureté, il faut dépenser trop de forces et je suis foncièrement paresseux" (AH, 167) [for to achieve a certain pitch of impurity one must expend too much energy. And I am fundamentally lazy MH, 142]. More wilfully, Baudelaire posited the need for "concentration," a centripetal counter to the "vaporisation" of God-the-prostitute. His alternative is the Dandy, walled off from the crowd—inscrutable, impassive, impersonal. Leiris obliquely invokes Baudelaire's exemplary figure of modernity by concluding L'Age d'homme with a dream, where he explains to a female friend "comment il est nécessaire de construire un mur autour de soi, à l'aide du vêtement" (AH, 226) [how necessary it is to construct a wall around oneself by means of clothing MH, 192]. The Dandy, like the Bohemian, is a new figure to emerge from the post-Revolutionary society where sons of the bourgeoisie did not renounce their class so much as try to sustain and extend its revolutionary legacy.[7] Baudelaire incarnated the

7. This is essentially the thesis developed by Gerrold Seigel in his reinterpretation of the bohemian phenomenon in nineteenth-century France. See his Bohemian Paris: Culture, Politics, and the Boundaries of Bourgeois Life 1830–1930 (New York: Penguin Books, 1986).

contradictory impulses of the bohemian rebel and poet Leiris described within his own oscillation between disgust and nostalgia. Generating their own mythologies, the romantic realists of the last century set the pattern of ambivalence characterizing most attempts to revise relations to the dominant class and ideology down to the present. This *déchirement* is correlated with the complicated attitude toward the working class any bourgeois must eventually confront within himself.

Toward the end of *L'Afrique fantôme* Leiris expresses relief at having killed off at least one juvenile myth—the voyage: "le mirage exotique est fini. Plus envie d'aller à Calcutta, plus de désir de femmes de couleur (autant faire l'amour avec des vaches: certaines ont un si beau pelage!)" (*AF*, 509) [the exotic mirage is over. Gone the desire for Calcutta, gone the wish for women of color (one might as well make love to cows: some have such beautiful fur!].[8] Despite many affinities with Baudelaire, he refuses *L'Invitation au voyage* because the fantasy of *luxe, calme et volupté* await him at home. Imagining himself in sumptuous clothes, taking tea at the Ritz, dancing with his wife, Leiris realizes that he will be accused of being a snob. More exactly, he retorts, "Je suis un enfant" (*AF*, 509) [I am a child]. And a propos of luxury in general, he confesses that it is glitter that really attracts him. But the serious issue is not to justify his own preferences; rather, it is the social connotations attached to luxury he deplores, so that the stratifications of bourgeois society have systematically denied workers access to it.

> Ce que je ne pardonne pas à la société bourgeoise, c'est la saleté des ouvriers. Tout luxe en est éclaboussé. . . . L'ouvrier, dénué de luxe, est à peine encore un homme; le bourgeois, monopolisateur du luxe, a le droit d'être un homme, mais de jour en jour son luxe devient plus

8. Leiris apologizes for any misunderstanding produced by this outburst by including the following reflection in his notes: "Guéri du 'mirage exotique'—ce qui, assurément, représentait un pas dans le sens d'une vue plus réaliste des choses—j'étais encore trop égocentrique pour ne pas céder au dépit. M'en prenant aux 'femmes de couleur' dont j'avais tant rêvé, je les ravalais maintenant par boutade au rang de vulgaires animaux, comme si l'amour fait avec quelqu'un sans nulle communication possible sur le plan du langage et dans des conditions telles qu'on ne peut être uni à lui par un minimum d'entente érotique n'avait pas toutes chances, en effet, de ne guère se différencier de la bestialité" (*AF*, 532) [Cured of the "exotic mirage"—surely a step in the direction of a more realistic view of things—I was nonetheless still too vain to not give in to spite. Taking it out on the women of color I had so often fantasized, I now lowered them to the rank of vulgar animals, as if lovemaking devoid of linguistic communication and with only a minimum of erotic compatibility, could not be distinguished from sheer bestiality.]

frelaté. *C'est pourquoi, en Europe, il faudrait tout changer.* [*AF*, 509–10, emphasis added]

What I cannot forgive bourgeois society is the filth of workers. All luxury is tainted by it. . . . Denied any luxury, the worker is barely a man; the bourgeois, monopolizing luxury, has the right to be a man, but every day his luxury becomes more vitiated. *Which is why in Europe, every thing must change.* [Emphasis added]

The slippage from luxury to revolution in a few brief sentences is not so surprising to readers familiar, as Leiris surely was, with Bataille's 1927 scatological analysis of class conflict entitled "l'Anus solaire": "Ceux en qui s'accumule la force d'éruption sont necessairement situés en bas. Les ouvriers communistes apparaissent aux bourgeois aussi laids et sales que les parties sexuelles et velues ou parties basses: tôt ou tard il en résultera une éruption scandaleuse au cours de laquelle les têtes asexuées et nobles des bourgeois seront tranchées"[9] [Those in whom the forces of eruption accumulate are necessarily located below. The communist workers appear to the bourgeoisie as ugly and as dirty as the hairy or base sexual parts: sooner or later this will lead to a scandalous eruption in the course of which the noble and asexual heads of the bourgeois will be severed].

Bataille had not yet published his more substantive mediations on the place of luxury within his general theory of expenditure, but one can assume some exchanges on the subject between the close friends. The centrality of these issues is further evidenced in Bataille's deconstruction of the surrealist model of revolutionary ideology and practice. Leiris, we recall, formulated his own rebellion by invoking the Promethean and Icarian examples which both incur some form of punishment, including symbolic castration. Thus, in his polemic with Breton, Bataille points out how the surrealists recapitulate earlier romantic revolutionary models, and even that of Nietzsche. The pattern is the same: seeking to express disaffection from his milieu of origin, the bourgeois attempts to establish solidarity with the "lower" classes by first aligning himself with marginal, potentially subversive and heterogeneous forces, whether dreams, eroticism, the irrational, or the workers themselves. Very quickly, however, the rebellion seeks legit-

9. Georges Bataille, *Oeuvres Complètes Premiers écrits* (1922–40). Présentation de Michel Foucault (Paris: Editions Gallimard, 1970), vol. 1, 85–86. Translations are my own.

imation through "superior" values, such as a "surreal," "spirit," or "absolute," even if it means spiritualizing the material phenomena derived from the margins of the social hierarchy. Most obviously, the idealist deviation appropriates traditional symbols such as the eagle, to the point of creating a mythological "sureagle" for itself. When the goals of class warfare are occulted, bourgeois rebels are misled into an idealistic, Icarian version of revolutionary illumination. Bataille cites the political icon of the eagle, which has entered into an alliance with the sun and castrates any attempt to undermine its authority (cf., Icarus, Prometheus, the Mithraic bull). Significantly, Bataille does not flatly condemn the recuperation since he recognizes, to some degree, its inevitability. With the example of Nietzsche, he concedes that

> la seule possibilité d'émancipation pour l'individu de la classe bour-
> geoise résulte de l'action éventuelle d'un complexe icarien. Il est im-
> possible de trahir sa classe par amitié pour le prolétariat, mais seule-
> ment par goût d'arracher ce qu'il faut bien appeler "feu du ciel,"
> conformément à une terminologie proprement nietzschéenne; et cela
> par simple subversion, pour le plaisir d'enfreindre des lois prétendues
> intangibles.[10]

> The only means of emancipation from his class for a bourgeois indi-
> vidual derives from the action prompted by an Icarian complex. It is
> impossible to betray one's class out of solidarity for the proletariat, but
> only out of the desire to steal the "fire from the sky," in keeping with a
> properly Nietzschean terminology; and even this is accomplished by
> means of simple subversion and because of the pleasure to transgress
> supposedly intangible laws.

This concession is made despite his acknowledgment that most bourgeois are attracted to rebellion the way moths flit to the light and bring
about their own destruction. Bataille's main target, the surrealist
claim to seek a point transcending "old" antinomies, is used to illustrate the modern version of the archaic deviation whereby "low" and
heterogeneous phenomena are appropriated and then sublimated into
"higher," immaterial ones. Needless to add, the surrealist act—a willingness to shoot at random, preferably into a crowd—is derided as
proof of the castration complex "ayant pour but d'attirer sur soi un

10. Georges Bataille, *Oeuvres Complètes Ecrits posthumes* (1922–40). (Paris: Gallimard, 1970), vol. 2, 99.

châtiment brutal et immédiat" (*OC* 11, 103.) [whose goal it is to bring upon oneself harsh and immediate punishment].

Bataille's last word on the matter is consistent with his generally extreme positions during this period—the only viable negativity is a base materialism in complete rupture with any vestiges of a dialectic of recognition. The bourgeois must agitate in concert with other groups and cannot establish himself as representative of any other class. With considerable acuity he points out that the impulses leading toward lower as well as higher values are at work in every milieu, but the political reality is that the bourgeoisie alone can claim the realm of ideas as its own. All representations thus emanate from "above."

Finally, it is relevant to note that despite references to Freud's recently published work on group psychology, Bataille's idiosyncratic tracts on the psychological structure of fascism, like the ideological critique just summarized, reject either phenomenological or psychoanalytic methods in order to privilege *états vécus*. At other moments Bataille invokes the examples supplied by French sociology, especially those of Mauss, where the allegedly irrational or symbolic basis of social life observed in other cultures provides an alternative vantage point from which to observe one's own. A few years later, along with Caillois and Leiris, Bataille organized a *Collège de sociologie* determined, among other goals, to explore "les points de coïncidence entre les tendances obsédantes fondamentales de la psychologie individuelle et les structures directrices qui président à l'organisation sociale et qui commandent ses révolutions" (*Collège*, 34) [the points of coincidence between the fundamental obsessive tendencies of individual psychology and the principal structures governing social organization and in command of its revolutions (*CS*), 11]. As dissident surrealists, they cautiously avoided positing a privileged *sur* position[11] while projecting the possibility for a new topos, a sacred sociology where the traditional oppositions—social VS. political, individual VS. collective, contemplative VS. activist—could be radically revised.

Historically, Leiris pursued these issues with greatest insistence. During the Collège years (1937–39) he was critical of Bataille's disregard for the rules of sociological method, and even more so of his exclusive emphasis on the "left" sacred.[12] Following the war, he opted

11. The exception would be Caillois's description of a *"sursocioalisation."* See Collège anthology, op. cit, 83 [36, translation].

12. Communicated in a personal interview September, 1983.

to contribute to Sartre's *Les Temps modernes* rather than Bataille's less visibly engaged *Critique;* he denounced the Algerian War and colonialism in general, and continued an official career as ethnologist, dutifully dividing his working hours between the autobiographical journals written at home and the professional monographs produced in his cell-like office at the *Musée de l'Homme.* At the age of 68, in the fourth and final volume of *La Règle du jeu, Frêle bruit,* he laments still being haunted by the apparently unresolvable tension between the exigencies of the voice within, and the call for political activism without, "rude épreuve pour qui l'affronte en poussant l'oubli de soi aussi loin qu'il le peut mais, en aucun cas, n'acceptera de mettre en veilleuse ses capacités critiques . . . " [harsh test for the individual who confronts it by pushing the neglect of self as far as possible while refusing to suspend faculties . . .].[13]

Without denying the existential anxiety to which this tension attests, one must nonetheless challenge its underlying assumptions. Indeed, why does activism constitute any more of an act of faith than writing? Conversely, how does the introspection of autobiography keep the critical faculty more alert than immersion into the outside world? Leiris exempted this opposition from his repudiation of the many "manichéismes puérils" constitutive of his daily dramas. His recognition of the relative fluidity within the inside/outside opposition notwithstanding, it is clear that the distinction highlights an inner struggle whose intensity is belied only by the banality of the terms themselves.

At stake in Leiris's formulation is the critical validity of the difference, and even conflict, between two modes of thinking and writing it appears to reinforce. Pitted against each other are the moments of poetic insight and sacred intensity which nourish the autobiographical literary writing, and the profane prose of the ethnographic studies targetting racism and colonialism. An alternative view, presented here, considers the prevalence of the sacred as an indication of its function as an *analytical* rather than purely descriptive category. The experiences related to or subsumed by the sacred are characterized as ambivalent and transgressive, defying the logic of noncontradiction to which the Western logos ostensibly obeys. However, unlike the African collective ceremonies described by Leiris, their significance is not universally recognized and the task of their interpretation now falls to individuals.

13. Michel Leiris, *Frêle bruit, La Règle du jeu* (Paris: Gallimard, 1976), vol. 4, 389.

Even mythological figures derived from biblical and classical antiquity have acquired a psychoanalytic meaning which Leiris rejects in order to restore to them their sacred function as mediating figures with the great forces of death and eroticism. In *Frêle bruit,* the sacred seems to have been displaced by a more profane and moderate mode of revelation, "le merveilleux." Leiris himself notes that the privileged objects or sites of his later experiences are all inanimate, fixed in an immobility which enhances their function to be "seen," apparently in contradiction with his own initial definition that they be "mêlé à la vie et non parqué dans un domaine abstrait *(FB,* 376) [immersed in life and not isolated into an abstract realm]. Other examples also omit any reference to the erotic, apparently justifying the claim that the sacred has been eclipsed. Yet Leiris's observation is followed by a digression on the erotic which underscores an essential feature of the sacred—its otherness, "sans commune measure avec le reste, et détaché insolemment du quotidien . . . " [without any common ground with all the rest, and brazenly detached from everyday life *(FB,* 339)]. The example he uses to justify this description is the same as in his 1938 presentation to the Collège regarding the sacred in everyday life—the juxtaposition of nude dancers at a nightclub, so close to the bourgeois spectators, yet separated by their "éblouissante crudité" *(FB,* 339). Similarly, the segregated quarters of the brothel are seen as

> si éloigné du monde tantôt trop affairé, tantôt trop vide de la rue bien qu'elle n'en soit séparée que par un simple seuil, matérialisation du tabou qui frappe le mauvais lieu. Règne païen, opposé au règne chrétien de la morale et qui, relevant du Sabbat plutôt que de la messe, appartient au merveilleux, non seulement parce que son éclat émerveille, mais parce que les règles y sont nulles et non avenues, travail et calcul hors de propos et qu'ayant pour axe la transe, où la lucidité s'évanouit, il représente la déchirure de la vie courante où l'illimité fait irruption. [*FB,* 339]

> so isolated from the sometimes too harried world, sometimes too deserted street, even though it is separated by a simple threshold, a materialization of the taboo placed upon the house of ill repute. Here the pagan reigns, opposed to Christian morality, closer to the Sabbath than to the Mass, and belongs to the marvelous not only because its radiance shines, but because all rules are null and void, work and calculations inappropriate, because it belongs to the realm of trance where reason evaporates, and because it represents the breach in everyday life where the infinite bursts forth.

But even if Leiris now approaches the marvels of eroticism through the passionless intermediaries of holy places, the quality of the experience it implies has not diminished in intensity. Like Proust, Leiris recognizes that the encounter with *le merveilleux* occurs through a complex dialectic entailing submission as well as the projection of force and desire (just as he described the power of the fetish) onto some object, place, or person. The sacred, Durkheim insisted, is not intrinsic but added on, and like love or power exists only to the extent the beholder wishes. In love as in Revolution, a complicity with other(s) is sustained by a common belief and total agreement in shared goals: thus, "merveilleux, poésie, amour, n'existent que si je m'ouvre, sans marchandage, à quelque chose—événement, être vivant, objet, image, idée—que mon désir d'illimité coiffe d'une auréole durable ou momentanée" (FB, 341) [the marvelous, poetry, love, only exist if I open my self without calculation, to some thing—an event, a living being, an object, image or idea—that my desire for infinity coiffs with a momentary or enduring nimbus]. Bataille claimed that an aura was created through impersonal instances of sovereign expenditure. Leiris, closer to Proust, discovers that the *merveilleux* is nourished at home, through roots which retract their wandering tendrils to dig deeper "au plus profond de nous (là où gisent et parfois s'agitent nos vrais secrets, ceux que nous ne connaissons trop confusément pour être en mesure de les divulguer) . . . (FB, 359) [to the innermost depths of our being (to that place where our true secrets rest and sometimes are stirred up, those which we ourselves know too confusedly to be able to divulge them . . .]. Chance may play a role in the encounter, but it occurs only on a terrain cultivated for its eventuality. One therefore understands that a sort of predestination is at work in order to allow the anticipated revelation to blossom from the memory traces of an intimate folklore sheltered and nourished for some time. The *merveilleux* thus springs from an "internal festival" or a "simple superlative" used to designate privileged events to be lived like an immediate and complete adhesion devoid of any religious supports, at the limit of life and at the confines of art (FB, 363). Rather than emanating from the sense of lack Bataille claimed as the motive for an expenditure which moves the individual toward others in a search for community, Leiris seeks to make the marvelous his, despite a haunting fear of solipsism, of isolation or of missed sharing, reminiscent of his earlier mortifying experiences of paralysis and impotence: "le merveilleux, dépasse-t-il pour moi ce sur quoi un esthète peut se complaire à rêvasser . . . " (FB, 373) [does my version of the marvelous go beyond the fantasies that a true esthete can indulge?]. Having resisted any confining characterization of the marvelous, Leiris concludes that his quest would culminate in a glorious unshackling of the chains he has dragged *de mer en mer*, bringing "l'impression d'être soudain délivré de tout ce qui m'oppresse . . . " (*FB*, 377) [the impression of sudden deliverance from all that continues to oppress me . . .]. But even the fantasy is tainted with guilt if the promised liberation remains a solitary and only momentary euphoria.

Bataille used the sacred to gauge the demise of collective experience in the modern world in his search for social forms capable of mediating the individual's confrontation with the terrifying and absolute separation represented by death. Leiris seems to impute a personal deficiency to his reticence to move beyond the confines of individual being in order to partake of a collective effort and to make a mark in history. Beyond their close friendship, they met on the common ground of a "collège," where the notion of a sacred sociology held out the possibility of reconsidering the intersections of the individual and the collective, the social and the political. Bataille was particularly intent on explaining the lack of a spontaneous mass movement in France at the time (1937) which would have countered the collective paralysis induced among individuals terrified by the prospect of imminent war and possible death. Similarly, we have seen how an appreciation of the sacred links the intimate revelations of the bourgeois Leiris as young Dandy and rebel to his adult public persona. By tracing the evolution of a *sensibilité* responsible for political *prises de position* as well as aesthetic choices, it is now possible to appreciate the general anthropology Leiris initially proposed.

In the *prière d'insérer* to accompany *L'Afrique fantôme* Leiris justified the extreme subjectivism of his work as leading to objective truths (213). Certainly universal insights occur, as when this critic of colonialism momentarily understand, to the point of implementing, the mentality of the average *colon* (*AF*, 225) and later notes without comment on the presence of feudal social relations among the indigenous Africans themselves. Jean Jamin has pointed out that Leiris included *L'Afrique fantôme* and the short essay on the sacred in everyday life in his application to the CNRS for a research position. He takes this as evidence that Leiris considered them examples of his general anthropology. What I am arguing here is that *L'Age d'homme* should also be regarded as an exemplary contribution to the development of an ethnographic mode of self-examination which is total to the extent to which it shows the bridges between the different levels of being that more orthodox sociologists and psychologists would isolate into discrete categories. This documentation of the incursion of the social into the personal has become a distinctive trait of French writing, both literary and within the human sciences. Less obviously, it has ethical and political consequences that sociologists have begun to explore and document.[14] In the case of Leiris, I believe that it poses an alternative way of approaching the dichotomization between his writing modes and the split between writing itself and some form of activism. Bataille's polemic with Breton was introduced for two reasons: first, because it demystifies the complex nature of political involvement among would-be defectors from the bourgeoisie and explores the unconscious factors determining the pattern of that involvement; second, because it anticipates the recognition that the deconstruction of collective representations constitutes the primary responsibility of the bourgeois intellectual.[15] Without denying the importance of making straightforward statements of support and adhesion to various causes, the most radical advances of recent scholarship have demonstrated that an essential component in the fight for social justice is the understanding of the roots of sexism, racism and class bias within the ruling milieus themselves, e.g., the myths, *phantasms*, complexes, linguistic tics, and so on, with which Leiris's everyday ethnography is concerned. To this end, Leiris, with characteristic modesty and unburdened of theoretical baggage, made a contribution in ways that neither he nor even some of his admirers fully appreciated.

14. See, for instance, the work of Pierre Bourdieu, especially *La Distinction* (Paris: Les Editions de Minuit, 1979).

15. For a discussion of the relevance of the Breton/Bataille polemic to contemporary issues in ethnography and literature, see Steven Webster, "The Historical Materialist Critique of Surrealism and Postmodernist Ethnographic Forms," in *Modernist Anthropology: From Fieldwork to Text*. Marc Manganaro, ed. (Princeton: Princeton University Press, 1990), 266–99.

MARC BLANCHARD

"'N stuff . . . ": Practices, Equipment, Protocols in Twentieth-Century Ethnography

A novelist narrates a plot. A poet writes verses. An ethnographer describes practices. Of all the writers in the French language Leiris is one of the more skilled at describing the world of persons and objects in terms of practices—actions performed more than once, often every day, in a social context with the purpose of modifying relations between subjects and objects with significant advantage.[1] In a beautiful passage of *Frêle bruit*, he talks about old country kitchens whose quaint charm is not unlike that of attics, coach houses (*"remises"*) and lean-to's, which, like grandmothers, tell the tales of the generations which have used them (Leiris uses the folk term: "mère-grand" [granny] or [grand-ma]): "Cuisine sans âge, artisanale en dépit de son équipement et qui, moins pudique qu'elle ne l'est quant à ses récipients, balais, torchons, serpillières, attirail de cirage, boîte à outils, etc., aurait le charme jamais épuisé de ces greniers ou remises qui, telles des mères-grands, racontent tant d'histoires aux enfants!" [An ageless kitchen, primitive in spite of its modern equipment, less chaste than its recipients, brooms, dish towels, mops, waxing materials, tool boxes, etc., might have the eternal charms of those attics or pantries, which like old grannies tell children so many stories!][2]

What one uses to make something, which can become an insepara-

1. I am following Bourdieu's general line on *practice* (see in particular: *Le Sens pratique* [Paris: Minuit, 1980], 87–109).
2. Michel Leiris believes in the power of female myths (the famous Judith and Lucrezia in *Manhood*) and mythical places, like kitchens, homes, inhabited by a female presence, even if Leiris continues to hold a masculine gaze on the accessories of the female body and female beauty (*Le Ruban au cou d'Olympia* [Paris: Gallimard, 1981]). Hereafter cited in the text.

YFS 81, *On Leiris,* ed. Blanchard, © 1992 by Yale University.

ble part of the practice itself since the artisan and the worker could hardly be what they are without the tools of their trade, is of central importance to the whole Leirisian *oeuvre.* The writer, poet, diarist, ethnographer, card filer and indexer, could not perform his work without his *equipment.* But the Leirisian equipment is exactly that: pieces of memory, elements of the past, fragments of dreams, but also pots and pans, pieces of gear, nondescript "fourbis," "attirail," "boîte à outil"—all the stuff that Leiris, much like Robinson, cannot do without, the former to write his books, the latter to grow, to hunt and to cook his food, and teach Friday—both to live the story of their lives. The names of the objects and equipment are hard to pin down because they are part and parcel of the Leirisian enterprise of holding the past together with the present, of finding a use for the vast array of things which constitute daily life. The issue is not what it was for Proust, to reconstitute with infinite patience a buried, all-encompassing perspective in the world of art, but to take an inventory of and to put to use what is around. In this case, because the user is a writer, the stuff, the gear is made up of words and the whole Leirisian enterprise is essentially linguistic. But because the practical side of life is mediated by the signs of language, whether they are songs, stories, or poems, Leiris invites us to learn the signs of experience, the ideas of objects one may have in one's head through his work with language. In the end, the enterprise is not simply modernist in the sense of an Ezra Pound or a James Joyce liberating the language from the constraints of a formalist lexicon and syntax; it is essentially postmodern, in that it seeks constantly to rehistoricize the present by retreading the past, adapting to circumstances, while also recasting one's entire perspective in a new way.

It is mostly in the fourth and last part of the *Règle du jeu* and in his papers, articles, presentations, reviews, many of which were collected in 1966 in the volume entitled *Brisées,* that Leiris takes up the question of equipment. He may still, here and there, as at the beginning of the *Règle du jeu,* care about elaborating a plan for living, a map of his existence, or justifying his strategy, as he does toward the end of *Frêles bruits* with reference to Nietszche and Sartre.[3] But the latter part of his

---

3. *Frêle bruit* (Paris: Gallimard, 1976), 309: "La 'Règle du jeu', au sens où je l'entends, c'est le mien système de valeurs (voir Nietzsche) ou le choix originel (voir Sartre) auquel doit répondre le jeu, conforme à mes goûts et à mes aptitudes, que je mènerai avec rigueur et cohérence." Hereafter cited in the text.

work is also interesting in that, Leiris, older and always closer to death, attempts there to make sense of things *out* of their historical perspective. Freed from the narrative imperative of going back to the source, his childhood, in *Brisées, Le Ruban au cou d'Olympia* and *A cor et à cri* Leiris follows the Mallarmean example of the "pièce de circonstance." Focussing on vignettes and less concerned with the narrative flow, the writer attempts, in a limited environment and without following a chronological development, to bring back the memories that now sollicit him out of the past. Reflecting on the May '68 revolution in Paris, in which he was more than a passive spectator, he sees banners everywhere. And those writings, taken out of their historical context, are the occasion for historicizing reflection. Now silent on the wall from which these banners jump at the oblivious passerby, they ask what the intellectual did or did not do during his life. They expose the pettinesses of life in an uncanny slogan. But they also need to be reexamined. The grandiose and Romantic beliefs they convey may have to be exposed and their perspective rearticulated (for instance, he is disenchanted with Castro's Cuba). What does a life amount to, when it is stripped of the existential engagement that gave it substance and meaning? Once the illusion that one lives *for* something has been explained away, what is it that remains of a lifestyle, a practice, a destiny?—A device, a configuration of language and power too faint to be reactivated but one that can at least be rethought, essayed in another way, perhaps. How to make sense of the devices for living? If they are "modèles réduits" [scaled down models], one needs to ask of what (*Frêle bruit*, 384). But Leiris chooses instead to ask the practical question par excellence. Not why? but how? Reflecting on the possibilities of a phrase with which he is obsessed (*fruit à la tête*), he asks himself about the conditions under which things work and sometimes don't [*inopérantes*] (*Frêle bruit*, 384ff.).

Brisées: literally broken pieces or parts, generally twigs and boughs, and metaphorically, tracks, both on the ground and in the ground, of what the forester, the lumberjack leaves on his way through the forest.[4] Shying away from the perspective which would explain Life, give Meaning to a quest, the writer now retrenches and seeks to

4. Even though it is probably a coincidence, and it is likely that Leiris has not read or cared for Heidegger, it is worth remembering that one of Heidegger's more seminal works is entitled *Holzwege*, pointing to the tracks left in the ground and orienting the walker, enabling him to find his way and to develop a strategy for following the tracks or on the contrary to go backward.

deal with the remnants, the leftovers—memories which are parts of books, of pictures, of organisms and bodies lying in his way. For the description of such parts, he has been inspired by poetry, the violence and the blazing of Rimbaud; by the painters, the staging of the quotidian in Picasso; and by Surrealists and fellow travelers, first among them, Marcel Duchamp, to whose *opérations* Leiris is particularly attuned. Fascinated by "dispositifs" [apparatuses] which make things work in a third way beyond what is possible and impossible, permitted and forbidden, Leiris admires Duchamp's "ready-made": objects whose reference can no longer be fixed and whose surprising or baffling interpretation often requires the reexamination or dismissal of established social conventions. The possibilities in this are endless. Via Duchamp, Leiris offers here the lineaments of an antiaesthetic with which to shortcircuit reason and deflect the obsession with clarity and transparence. A new field is opened to the philosopher, the epistemologist, and the writer hoping to constitute his writing as a new discipline in the margins:

Une fois liquidé le grand art, une fois l'homme exorcisé de sa confiance candide en le discours, la place resterait nette pour l'édification d'une nouvelle *physique* (ou *logique*) *amusante*, ouverte aux solutions élégantes de quelques ARTS ET METIERS[5]

Once great art has been eliminated, once man has been exorcised of his frank confidence in speech, there would be room for the construction of a new *physics* (or *logic*) *for fun*, open to the elegant solutions of some ARTS and CRAFTS. [107]

—the writer also hoping to engineer constructions whose blueprints are never clear but which seem to function nonetheless in a mysterious and anonymous way:

Espèce de jeu de marelle—sur un terrain d'apparence bénigne mais creusé un peu partout de fondrières métaphysique—, suite problématique de domaines que la raison ne peut parcourir qu'à cloche-pied, tel est le genre d'images auquel il semblerait, en gros, qu'on puisse se référer pour rendre compte du type d'opérations à quoi Duchamp s'est

5. *Brisées* (Paris: Gallimard, 1966), 119; *Broken Branches*, trans. Lydia Davis (San Francisco: North Point, Press 1989). A reference to the science of making (art) and manufacturing (métier), as well as to the famous Parisian Science Museum by the same name. Hereafter cited in the text.

attaché dans nombre de ce qu'il faut bien, faute d'un mot plus com-
mode, intituler ses 'oeuvres.' [*Brisées*, 118]

A sort of hopscotch—on a patch of ground that appears benign but
is pitted all over with metaphysical potholes—a problematic series of
domains that reason can travel over only by hopping, such is the sort of
image to which it would seem, in sum, that one could refer to understand the type of procedures Duchamp has adopted in a number of what
we must call, for lack of a more convenient word, his "works." [106]

What lies behind the construct, however? The writer as contractor,
sometimes a *deus ex machina* on the scaffolds of rhetoric, at other
times, a mole endlessly boring through the underground tunnels of a
subtext ("une taupe qui fore ses galeries")? (*Le Ruban*, 157). The book is
but a "pauvre panoplie," (*Le Ruban*, 156) articulated on the index
cards, the "fiches" Leiris has continued to fill during his whole life in
the field of ethnography, mornings in his office at the Musée de
l'Homme or afternoons at his desk in his Parisian home. Could it be
that the quest for an authentic self, which had so long constituted the
ethical imperative, the governing rule (the *règle du jeu*) for his writing
career, for his life in general, was nothing more than the reflection of
scaffolds and trestles, theatrical props at best? And yet this reflection, a
mere image, a duplication of a preexisting reality, is also inhabited,
"lived" in. Leiris hesitates between the "pauvre panoplie," completely
lacking in human persona and devoid of meaning, and something substantive, the matter of language:

. . . je regarde mes écrits comme la fragile carapace que je me bâtis avec
les mots que j'ai reçus tout faits et que mon industrie traite de son
mieux (mots dont l'alignement sur le papier reproduit l'itinéraire sinu-
eux et haché que trace non sans rejets, repos et retouches ma main
munie d'une plume et dans le labyrinthe duquel j'avance à pas précau-
tionneux comme si, doutant de mes lumières, j'attendais de cette
plume qu'elle me guide en me tenant par la main), la logique veut que
j'habite ces écrits, faute de quoi ils ne seraient que coques vides et,
plutôt que les pièces d'une armure, une pauvre panoplie dont, comme
un enfant qui s'en est amusé, je laisserais les éléments épars autour de
moi. [Ibid.]

I look upon my writings as the fragile carapace that I build with the
words given to me ready-made, but which I strive to handle as well as
possible (words whose alignment on paper reproduces the sinuous and

intermittent itinerary that my hand with pen traces with rejections, pauses, and corrections; in the labyrinth in which I proceed cautiously as if in doubt about my insights, I was waiting for the pen to guide me by holding my hand). Logic insists that I inhabit these writings, without which they would be mere empty shells, and rather than pieces of armor, they would be a poor soldier's outfit whose scattered elements I would abandon around me as a child who had played with them.

Is it a game of mirrors ("A moins que tout ceci ne soit qu'un jeu de métaphores . . . ") [unless all this is a mere play of metaphors . . .] or something else: a representation performed by the writer completely adhering to his role and transfigured by it? ("entrer dans la peau de son propre rôle")? (ibid.).

The litany of famous writers hailing from famous paintings or photographs goes from Homer with his blind stick to Kafka wearing a bowler à la Magritte (*Le Ruban*, 158). It is as though all these famous people were characters we couldn't remember without the attribute with which they have been immortalized. Their public image is for Leiris an analogue of what happens to him when he is trying to write a self-portrait. His own image falls into the public domain. What will *they* remember him by? Those who don't know him like Montaigne's relatives? In writing he uses the "je" and the "il" as the two faces of the *mask* which he has constructed but which also *makes* his face (". . . il n'étant ici qu'un masque derrière lequel, parlant de ce qu'il eût été plus décent de taire, je me suis dissimulé . . . " (*Le Ruban*, 163). When the book is written and read and the writer, for all intents, dead (and even before it is written, is not the writer, in Blanchot's words, also dead to himself?). The process looks like a *protocol*, not a thing but a practice that we are supposed to know, which governs everything else we know and whose function is to appoint, to authorize reality, to order it for us, so that we may also live in it ("ne peut pas faire illusion . . . ") [ibid]. The writer's function is to activate this protocol and the readers', to participate in the ceremony. First it is a gift of poetic colors to highlight a life rich in dreams, reveries and fantasies. Not an escape, a way to overcome death, but a way to seek relief from the oppressive, insignificant personhood of everyday life. Through the *"dispositif"*, the *"protocole,"* revealed and operated by the writing ritual, an individual existence is made culturally aware of itself and autobiography becomes ethnography.

The Leirisian challenge resides in the recall of a memory which would bring into being the unfolding of a narrative without expressly relying on the diary mode. In a passage of *RO*, Leiris asks himself how to account for a phrase that occurred to him, as he lies barely awake in the early morning hours, In trying to solve the enigma, he speaks of a "theater of operations," (*Le Ruban*, 172), where operating on language with the tools of etymology and phonology makes him confront something more *real* and present ("non pas un fantôme, mais l'épaisseur vivante d'une présence"). The practice is intense, the practitioner intent on writing, pushing the pen ("appuyant et prenant appui sur ma plume,") (ibid), while he remains frustrated by the experience of having to *transfer* his ideas to paper, when what he really wanted was to inscribe his thoughts on the surface of his body, so completely and without interruptions that it would have been entirely covered with signs. Writing on paper is like tattooing, an operation, a procedure, by which life can be imprinted. But not quite, because the process is also nothing if not mechanical, daily, quotidian, and ritual and the only way to signify is to employ an already existing language, which everyone understands, even if it means very little. "Conversation: la plupart du temps, broutilles qu'on se passe et repasse comme des pièces de monnaie ou des marchandises qu'on troque" (*Le Ruban*, 174). The irony is that the object of writing is to give meaning to "life," and that it can only do that with a model, a configuration, a lifelike protocol of writing, albeit not life itself. For a *true* conversation shouldn't be simply a bartering process: "Communiquer n'est pas un troc (affaire d'échange ou de donnant-donnant) . . . " (*Le Ruban*, 178). But which is it? Is it or is it not exchange? On the one hand, conversation is simply the disposition of locutors and their interchange. On the other, it is also the spark that is ignited from their conjunction. But the *dispositif*'s function is just that: to connect and to ignite the spark when the proper noun, the verb, has been invented, coined, inscribed in the text.

The *dispositif*, the *configuration* and generally the cohort of Leirisian phrases referring to the setup of representation within language all speak to a sense of the rule, the structure already laid out, as well as to the potential of a more special poetic language. In this Leirisian essay, one can certainly see a symbolic replaying of the opposition between a common day standard language and a truly poetic language, but also a playing out of the anthropology and the ethnopoetics of language. On the one hand, language *is* related to a social practice, and it is itself action (more than once Leiris argues for a writing, an *écriture*, which would have the same force as an act in the world). This is an old nostalgia of the poets and the novelists: to make literature speak, to make the text change the world. A nostalgia, by the way, which has had a hard time surviving the Marxist ethic that the whole point is not to describe the world but to change it. And on the other hand, it suggests a certain kind of practice, not really in the world, but one which *might come into* the world through the words, the phrases enacting it.

This is not too far from the "hasard objectif" vaunted by the Surrealists, where the writer seeks to reconstitute as social or cultural practices events with no apparent coherence or relevance to him. Toward the end of *Le Ruban au cou d'Olympia,* Leiris describes for us a famous genre painting "The Dogon in a Gondola," in which we can imagine a swarthy African oddly riding a gondola on the Grand Canal. As we read on, we find that the famous painter is actually Leiris himself reconstructing one of his most memorable daydreams and fashioning for us a scene where the subjects of his ethnographic mission to the Dogons and to Gondar in his *Phantom Africa* are reinterpreted along the lines suggested by his friend the Surrealist writer Raymond Roussel, who died in Italy (hence, Venice and gondolas). To this reconstruction, Leiris also summons the imaginary painting that another Surrealist friend, Pierre Klossowski, *might* have painted, had he wanted to illustrate his own fantasy of a revolutionary Minerva leading the riotous Parisians against the Right and the Germans during the 1871 Commune (hence the tricolor arrangement of the Dogon's accoutrement). Beside the obvious alliteration and the homophonic pun (Dogon/gondola/Gondar), the setup for the "Dogon en gondole" is thus entirely secondhand, equipmentlike. Neither the Roussel nor the Klossowski reference on which the imaginary painting in Leiris's daydream rests, is real. Itself a daydream reconstructed with the help of the daydreams of others, the "Dogon en gondole" is the product of an invention which sets up reality with a certain detachment. It makes it at one and the same time familiar, (something encountered before), and oddly irrelevant, (the overall picture is nothing if not a grid for discrete stories individually having nothing in common with each other). When they are put together, they seem to add up to something for which there is no single equivalent in the culture, but with which the subject, the portraitist identifies, albeit, at a strange remove, his own image as the Other, and perhaps a dead Other at that. Michel Leiris, the manipulator of memories, this time as Dogon or Gondar informant, is being carried almost unbeknownst to himself on the river of death on a strange land (what is stranger: a Dogon in Venice or Leiris in Gondar?).

That the point of this bizarre self-portrait is ethnographic and belongs to the conversational barter of which cultures in general and Leiris's own anthropology in particular are made, becomes clear when Leiris remembers having met again in Paris thirty years after the first trans-African expedition, his native Ethiopian informant for what has to become *Phantom Africa*. The man, who had come to Paris with another anthropologist in order to seek treatment for an ailment, told Leiris his answer to his wives who were asking him what he, so old, sick and decrepit, was going to do in Paris; "On meurt partout"] [*one dies everywhere*] (*Le Ruban*, 183). That is to say, the man from Gondar speaks of dying in Paris, just as Roussel killed himself in a hotel in Palermo: Leiris, dreaming of his Dogon in Venice and analyzing his own reverie, finds in the Venetian gondoliere the image of Charon, the captain of Death, ferrying the writer's soul across the Styx of his *écriture*.

This example is significant, if only because it shows how sets of associative memories can create a variable *dispositif*, set up a scene reconstructed from various fragments in the life of the individual subject and images or emblems which identify this individual as the product of multicultural interpretation. Leiris modestly presents his written fantasy as *genre painting*. But the interest of *genre painting* is precisely the act of shying away from the full-fledged narrative whose sole function would be to reinscribe the past thus affording the reader with a totalizing view of the past. The reader is thus granted a perfectly unobstructed view of history, a clear point of view on events, which sets itself up as a document to be interpreted purely on social and cultural grounds. The point is not to depict reality or to show it off, but to communicate the message that it is reducible to a practice. To understand the painting is to reconstruct the practice and to historicize it in the eye of the beholder, even though it may appear frivolous and timeless at first—a pure object for aesthetic contemplation. In the retranslation from the painting of imagination to the text of memory, the *generic* aspects of the representation (in this case, the imaginary painting is about death understood as a universal custom) illuminate the text/painting as a document to be recomposed and worked through ("comme tels artistes de notre époque qui donnent ainsi à entendre que l'oeuvre est avant tout un document") [*Le Ruban*, 180]. In the tradition of interpretive memory from Aristotle to Freud, the emphasis falls on the totalizing view provided by the memory operation; the wager is that through remembering, the entirety of the past can indeed be retrieved. Leiris's preference for a partial memory, whose design would remain loose, leaves him freer to articulate his text as the moment and the locus of the setup, thus also giving his reader the impression that the past is a painting, both "monumental" and on a small scale ("de petit format") (*Le Ruban*, 181), and that this painting is essentially "de genre." As in genre painting, it is incumbent upon the reader to recognize a generalist view of the world where the individual is identified by a familiar practice, the detail, the significance of which must sometimes be reestablished, explained anew. In this sense, the strategy of weaving the text around the *genre* object reaps more than one benefit: it universalizes the enterprise of self-portrait while also dissolving it into a cosmography where a life being lived can only be known to the extent that personal and autobiographical (all knowledge is an effect of the inscription of self into the world) is itself set up as an interpersonal, intercultural institution.[6]

In setting up the *dispositif* which produces autobiography or self-portrait, literary production is subverted by ethnographic arrangements, and those ethnographic dispositions are themselves laid out on a geological model. The self-portraitist of works, like the ethnographer of Dogon and Gondar, from his notes in the field and the description of personal institutions is constituted, like the ethnographic treatises, by the transfer, the transcribing of those *fiches* into a series or layers of narratives, providing extended, generic subtexts for the descriptions of individual practices. Much of what man believes in, lives by, and practices is superimposed onto previous beliefs and practices, forcing the social scientist to function like an archeologist taking a vertical view of the successive civilizations which have inhabited the interactive space he studies. There is in the latter part of Leiris's work, and perhaps even more pronounced as one moves away from the *Règle du jeu*, into the writings of the '70s and the '80s, a tendency to restrict the text to the vignette, sometimes the short cameo picture, perhaps illustrative in its very detail of a whole other narrative in progress (that of the postwar French intellectual seeking to identify himself in the blur of international capitalism and decolonization). But, although Leiris testifies time and again to his political options and already poignantly prefigures the post-Modern obsession with political correctness in the midst of an ever more rapidly changing world, this other narrative is to

6. On this, see J. B. Pontalis's famous text on Leiris: "Michel Leiris et la psychanalyse sans fin" (Paris: Gallimard, Idées, 1968), 313–35, pp. 128–44 in this issue.

a large degree, nonexistent.[7] What remains in the specific text, fixated in what we should now call the "fiche de circonstance" of an anthropologist who would have read Mallarmé, is a scene which no longer speaks to the memorialist rereading his notes: "Tout ceci—j'en suis mortifié—n'existe plus guère que par écrit. Je reprends, par exemple, ce que je disais de la servante Berthe, je le recopie presque mot pour mot, en me gardant du romantisme qui me pousserait à poétiser le modèle, mais ce n'est pas cela qui me permet de la revoir telle qu'elle était"[8] (*Le Ruban*, 180). [I am mortified that all this exists only in writing. For example, I look over what I said about Berthe, the maid, I copy it almost verbatim, refraining from the romanticism which would impel me to "poeticize" the model, but that does not enable me to see her again as she was].

There is certain irony in the fact that the writer of the end of the *Règle du jeu*, and the texts that follow it, continues to work with notes taken in the field, which he then incorporates into what is supposed to be a more elaborate, a more personal narrative, now that it is increasingly becoming clearer that a unitary, homogeneous self-definition of the subject of the text is impossible and if at all possible, at least impractical. It is also ironic that the vignettes in the later work produce as an effect of *genre* a practice, a performance that is no longer available. It no longer *speaks*, even as Leiris copies over the *fiche* into his new text, while remaining careful not to remake the original encounter. The notes read as though they had been written by someone else: "ces notes si peu parlantes qu'elles me semblent presque recenser les choses qu'un autre aurait vécues ou recueillies" (*Le Ruban*, 188) [these inexpressive notes so flat that they almost seem to enumerate things that someone else might have lived and gathered]. But another memory, spurred on by the first in the very labor of copying and processing the first memory, provides a new terrain for the investigation. Leiris has moved from one figure to another, from one style to the next, and the character he was striving to define—in this case a prestidigitator on tour in the smaller French Antilles—finally emerges

---

7. I am aware of the distinction between autobiography and self-portrait: one is personal and the other, cultural. But my point is not to show a distinction between literary genres but rather, to discuss the problematics of genre in an anthropological perspective.

8. The entire *Règle du jeu* series is peppered with such political testimonies, but the clearest, and the most famous, is perhaps Leiris's 1951 paper "L'Ethnographe devant le colonialisme," reprinted in *Brisées*, 125–45.

from his notes as a new specimen in a *herbarium:* "fragments d'un aide-mémoire où des choses enregistrées sur le vif ou peu s'en faut sont fixées comme dans un herbier et auquel je puis aujourd'hui me reporter," (*Le Ruban,* 180) [fragments of a memorandum to which I can refer back today, and where things are recorded live or nearly so and are fixed as in a herbarium]. Leiris peppers his memories with records of the populace's reaction to the illusionist. Most of those comments are the largely unfavorable opinions of the local people, to this outsider. They think he is a sham of a metropolitan Frenchman, condescending toward his ethnic audience. Later, on the boat back to Guadeloupe, Leiris catches sight of his man seasick over a barrel, throwing up, while the locals rejoice in revenge. That the whole passage recounts an episode of failed magic, precisely in one of the countries where Leiris had himself conducted his anthropological research, takes on a symbolic value in the search for a phenomenological difference. The shabby Eurocentric trickster being exposed is to his skeptical Third World audience what the notes are to the uncertain writer of *Le Ruban* wondering about his own powers to resuscitate the past. Yet the notes which don't speak and do not help the note taker to reinvent the world of which he was once a part (and which mesmerizes him somehow the way Manet's "Olympia" continues to fascinate him—she is naked, has nothing to offer except her complete nudity, and yet what invariably attracts the eye and titillates, is the fact that she wears a black band around her neck and mules on her feet), are to his new manuscript the *dispositif,* the context in which something, even something ridiculously inadequate but sobering as the natives' reaction to the tricks of the European charlatan, begins to come to life.

But to theorize the *dispositif* is to privilege the invariant, the structure, while neglecting the fact that for both Leiris and the first Lévi-Strauss whose *Tristes tropiques* Leiris is one of the first to welcome, the *dispositif* is *not yet* a structure, but rather still a part of the experience of living in the field and modifying it even as he seeks to describe it. The field, whether the Brazil of Lévi-Strauss or the Africa or the Caribbean of Leiris, is a pretext for the *bricoleur* on the move to orient himself in relation to the world around him, as he lets himself be guided as much by participation as by observation. In this phase where the anthropologist in the field first reacts to a series of practices, which he must first mimick before he can hope to explain them and make them rational at a remove, the order of the day is to identify and collect as much of what the surroundings suggest to sight, hearing, and memory. This collecting, in turn, raises, albeit without ever properly answering it, the question of transforming the participation into observation. It is at this junction, where anthropology wishes to be a science and realizes that it must first go through the steps of being a technique—in a text which points to the *bricoleur*, albeit without ever making him anything else but the facilitator of this process—that the *bricolage* finds its poetic and in the case of the Guadeloupe magician, its political epiphany.

The term "bricoler" is used by Leiris liberally. It speaks to him mostly of a solitary, an *idiotic* activity, in the ethnographic sense this word had for Diderot in *Rameau's Nephew*, while it also serves as a medium or transformer of the environment. It is the equipment, the *tool box* ["boîte à outils"] mentioned at the beginning of the *Règle du jeu*, which, "vade mecum de naufragé," [drowned man's vade mecum][9] will allow him to survive by exploiting all the resources of the linguistic realm, like a jobber, a handyman working with the limited resources at his disposal: "faire feu de tout bois." In this broad use of *bricolage*, Leiris is close to *Lévi-Strauss*. It is the move by which the writer of books lifts from the record of his experiences around the world configurations, topologies, *dispositifs*, which authorize him both to rewrite and to reread the past for blueprints and grids through which he can record what happened *and* imagine what could have happened with some degree of accuracy. Very much the *bricoleur* figuring out what should work and what shouldn't, Leiris strives for the "mot juste" and in addition to the vignettes which now take the place of an autobiographical narrative he feels he no longer has in him, he gives us pages of lists in the tradition of his Surrealist lexicon "Glossaire: j'y serre mes gloses" originally published in 1925: lists of words, of associations, of puns to jog the mind without a story to tell. The wordmaker has replaced the storyteller, the lexicographer, the autobiographer in a *bricolage* which makes clear the poetic function of language as it projects code and message together in curiously self-referential statements about the outside world. Therein lies the promise of a certain mastery: "la combinaison de mots, phrases, séquences, etc., que je suis seul à pouvoir bricoler . . ." (*Le Ruban*, 195) [The combination of words, sentences, sequences, etc. . . . which I alone can patch together]; a remedy capable of changing a situation and a life:

9. "Boîte à outils," *Biffures*, (Paris: Gallimard, 1948), 49; "vademecum," *Le Ruban*, 195.

"si je dois finir dans une solitude à laquelle je n'aurai pas le coeur d'apporter le catégorique remède" (ibid); [If I must end up in a solitude to which I won't have the heart/courage to bring the final solution] of an exchange, a barter. But the general promise to the writer, the Robinson Crusoe of the Modern Age, without the benefit of Friday or Bible on his island, is simply of survival: to survive in order to write and vice versa.

That the linguistic train of thought ("la combinaison des mots"), which is always Leiris's own, merges with the anthropological (*Robinson*), and then the existential, shouldn't come as a surprise. While the preoccupation with the end of the rope, death, is a constant of the *Règle du jeu*, this death can also be seen as the price one pays for severing language from its reference, its outer relation. Language in itself is nothing. And more than once, Leiris speaks to the lack of meaning of his representations, his reconstructions, when his remembering has in fact left him with nothing else than the sense of the ebb and flow of time. In the passage I have just quoted, without the pretext, the ongoing *bricolage*, Leiris-Robinson sees himself as a satiated lotus eater ("travaux nourriciers expédiés"), drifting into sleep and unable to face the sea, to anticipate and to hope—precisely perhaps because he might have used language in an ancillary way: in order, that is, to communicate something, to arrive somewhere. But Leirisian language is not subordinate, precisely because it explores and lives down the conditions of subordination. It wills itself as practice: "Qu'est-ce que, pratiquement, je poursuis?" (ibid). [What am I pursuing pragmatically?]

We meet here the conditions laid out by Lévi-Strauss in his *Savage Mind* for a definition of *bricolage* in contradistinction with pure science or even engineering.[10] *Bricolage* doesn't consider the state of the world and is not interested in goals. It only considers the means. Nature is not to be explicated nor is it to be reorganized in a grand manner—although the modifications effected by the *bricolage* operation will eventually cause the objects used in the operation to be realigned. As Lévi-Strauss has well shown, the *bricoleur* is constrained by the time, the history and the state of the language in which he works. Moreover, because the *bricoleur* always operates as a captive of his conditions, his products, his findings are good only once and for one

10. Claude Lévi-Strauss, "La Science du concret," *La Pensée sauvage* (Paris: Plon, 1962), 3–47; *The Savage Mind*, trans. George Weidenfeld and Nicolson, Ltd. (Chicago, University of Chicago Press, 1966), 1–33.

specific use only. There are many other characteristics of *bricolage*, all
of which Lévi-Strauss reviews thoroughly in the chapter "The Science
of the Concrete" at the beginning of the *Savage Mind*. Encouraged by
Leiris's own early review of *Tristes tropiques*[11] to weave the Leirisian
text around a Lévi-Straussian text, I am especially interested in net-
working and jobbering, (*bricoler*) the work of two anthropologists both
of whom by refining the linguistic medium end up putting their fieldwork to different use—the one, Lévi-Strauss using mythopoetic references to advance ethnographic paradigms and the other, Leiris using
field techniques to advance the cause of autobiography as a form of
ethnopoetics. It is more than a coincidence that Lévi-Strauss of both
Tristes Tropiques and the *Savage Mind* who resorts to poetic metaphors to reflect on the very way cultures can be made universally
significant and that, on the other hand, the Leiris who interests us is
the one who continues throughout his literary work, to hark back to
the techniques of the anthropologist, belong in the same discursive
formation. In the work of each, *bricolage* produces a redefinition of
the relation between language and reference. In Lévi-Strauss, and in
Tristes tropiques in particular, ethnographic work is made possible,
authorized, as it were, by combining considerations of geography and
geology with traits of personal autobiography. In Leiris the search for
personal traits produces a text where a self-image is essentially produced by multiple combinations of the cultural artefacts inventoried
by the writing subject. In both works, that of the early Lévi-Strauss and
of the later Leiris (or rather of the Leiris who, toward the end of his life,
returns to what he has always been, the dissident Surrealist poet of the
twenties and thirties), a comparative view of culture is enriched by a
reflection on associative models at work in everyday practice.

However, this epistemological framing of the comparative paradigm by its practical applications in the discourse of everyday life is
itself only a device, the grid, the *dispositif* governing all others in the
text, whose ontological status must eventually be queried.[12] But why

11. "A travers *Tristes tropique*," in *Brisées*, 199–209.
12. Lévi-Strauss states: "It is necessary to add that the balance between structure
and event, necessity and contingency, the internal and external is a precarious one. It is
constantly threatened by forces which act in one direction or the other according to
fluctuations in fashion, style or general social conditions (*The Savage Mind*, 30). Leiris
chimes in: Qu'est-ce pratiquement je poursuis?—La combinaison des mots, phrases,
séquences, etc., que je suis seul à pouvoir bricoler. . . . Ou plutôt ce qui me fascine,
c'est moins le résultat, et le secours qu'en principe j'en attends, que ce bricolage même
dont le but affiché n'est tout compte fait qu'un prétexte" (*Le Ruban*, 195).

is the writer so obsessed with finding personal, "subjective" meta-phors for the anonymous grid which articulates his images in the first place, if not because through it a voice speaks and a particular way of being, of configuring becomes apparent, or at least audible in the dis-course? The move from the visual to the auditory is not a philosophical capitulation. It is not a question of suggesting to the ear what the eye can't see. Both Lévi-Strauss and Leiris are fond of the musical reference at the point at which the visual paradigm fails. Besides praising the concept of serial composition as an image of the mythic segueing or *fugueing*, Lévi-Strauss "sees" a music of the voice in the midst of the most visible, geographic, or geological panorama. And Leiris praises voice as the only remaining significant aspect of a narrative every-where in disarray in his last work, *A cor et à cri*, published in 1988.

At the end of this double weaving or *métissage* of autobiography and anthropology as well as of one ethnopoetic and the other, we need to ask one last question: that of the relation of writing, *écriture*, to eth-nography in particular, but perhaps, more generally, that of the func-tion of writing in the empirical field of social practices. To the extent that they take place at a definite time in recent history, perhaps the beginning of the post-Modern moment, when the modernity, the new-ness of the writing project itself is questioned, the enterprise on both sides, of elaborating through what is clearly writing (*écriture*) and not simply the tabulation of quantitative data or a practical theory of lan-guage and cultural relations, both the experiences of Leiris and Lévi-Strauss are fundamental to our post-Modern epistemology. To the ex-tent that they raise the urgent question of the authenticity of the writing subject by showing how faint, how problematic his image remains, both works designate a political moment in the passage from Modernism to post-Modernism. Because of the shock of the encounter with the Other, reminiscent of Montaigne and Rousseau, especially the latter whom both Lévi-Strauss and Leiris hold in great esteem, it is clear that the search for self adumbrates the process of decolonization, to which both authors, and especially Leiris, can amply testify. *Tristes tropiques*, written in the nineteen fifties records an experience of the late thirties, and *Phantom Africa* (which was not reprinted until very recently and speaks of the first trans-African expedition of 1931) both mark the evolution of an anthropology of the Other in a colonial world which is fast becoming the Third World. In this sense, Leiris's nostalgic reference to Robinson and Friday is clear. But to the extent that the strategy of combining ethnography with monography at a time when the Rimbaldian dictum that "je est un autre" and especially in this case perhaps, "un autre Dogon," seems to hold sway, the enterprise of a certain Leiris and a certain Lévi-Strauss, taken both as ethnographers together rather than as anthropologists and poets separately, provides moving historical testimony to this last Romantic avatar, perhaps the ultimate genre painting, of the late twentieth-century writer working in the field of the Other, mixing his own voice, his own *mythos*, with that of an improbable native informant.

J. B. PONTALIS

Michel Leiris, or Psychoanalysis Without End*

All self-knowledge comes up against difficulties that have been signalled hundreds of times. The confusion between subject and object abolishes the minimal distance without which there is not even a gaze. The goal is indeterminate. Precisely what is one trying to grasp? A past of which one wishes to be the historian, a character one proposes to diagnose, or an unconscious whose treasures one hopes to excavate? The undertaking is ambiguous: is it an attempt at self-justification or a plea to be judged? An attempt to set oneself free, or to compromise oneself? An attempt at self-recuperation via a form or a value, or an attempt to escape oneself through words and images? The ambiguity means that readers of confessional literature are often in search of projections rather than portraits. If they want veracity they are more likely to place their trust in the biographer; they can go back to the legend, the statue and the grimaces later.

This feeling of unease becomes even more pronounced in diaries which, in extreme cases, claim to be able to record and preserve whole lives, and overlook the fact that even the drabbest life is defined, not by an admission of what has happened and complete respect for impressions, but by the complex and often invisible process whereby a field of existence and action is elaborated day by day. This is why, no matter what feelings are analysed, what decisions are taken or what circumstances are evoked, all diaries have certain features in common. Those

*Authorized translation of J. B. Pontalis, "La Psychanalyse sans fin" (Paris: Gallimard, Idées, 1968), with the permission of Gallimard and Associated Books, United Kingdom.

YFS 81, *On Leiris,* ed. Blanchard, © 1992 by Yale University.

features do not, as it is sometimes claimed, have anything to do with character-types. They relate to a certain bias.

Diaries make for exciting reading. We are going to see through all the role-playing and touch the 'real' man. We are going to discover, beneath an infinite diversity of facts, actions and states of mind, what it is that makes a life a unified totality. A specific responsibility will suddenly emerge from the day to day contact with events which obliterate the writer's personal path.

The hope is illusory, and the answer is disappointing. It is only in the interplay between mask and face, between mythology and visible history that we can see our 'real' man. As for unity, what unity can there possibly be, other than that of our actual undertakings? Ultimately, it is unreasonable to hope for anything more than a day to day commentary on a day to day life. Hence the sterile misery that provides so many diaries with their subject matter. Hence the sterile misery of any consciousness that tries to catch a glimpse of itself day by day, of the naive, distraught *ego* struggling—without doing itself too much harm—in a trap of its own making as it enjoys the delights of martyrdom. Difficulties, regrets, sighs, repetitions and the feeling of getting nowhere do not stop us from tirelessly trying to spy on ourselves by recording feelings, tastes and anecdotes. We look for decisive moments, set up crucial experiences. A waste of time. No matter how much consideration we show it, the monster refuses to emerge. How can I recognize myself as a whole person in this literally insane anger, in that ludicrous gesture? And how can I deny that they compromise me?

Diaries seem fated to be cyclomythic. Either I am enchanted by my inexhaustible wealth, or I am discouraged by my constantly reworked platitudes and have to confess my dismay. Why will this ego never put in a personal appearance? Those who do not achieve that degree of lucidity conclude: 'This is the way I am; that's how I am.' They objectify themselves by becoming characters, images or balance-sheets and believe that, having boldly confessed their failings and their strengths, they are on perfectly good terms with themselves.

One suspects Michel Leiris is not unaware of all these difficulties. The difference is that, instead of constantly being frustrated by them or giving up, he makes them the subject of his work, which suddenly takes on an exemplary value for the reader. What does it cost a man to devote himself unflinching to a task which seems both innocent and commendable (or at least highly recommended): self-investigation? The undertaking is ambiguous from the outset, and it becomes truly dizzying when we pursue it further. Anyone who doubts that has only to survey the path that led Leiris, with not a few stops and detours along the way, from *L'Age d'homme* (Leiris 1939) to *Fourbis* (Leiris 1955). It is because its ambitions are deliberately modest that *L'Age d'homme* is such a complete success. How can one fail to admire the distant but intimate way in which the author contemplates himself, feigning neither haughty indifference nor a passion for discovery. From the very beginning—remember how the book begins: 'I am just thirty-four; half a life' (Leiris 1939, 23)—the voice speaks from just the right place. Openly addressing itself to an audience, to others, trying to inform and not seduce them, it speaks of Leiris as though he were an other, one of them, one of us. It thus dispels the ever-present ambiguity that infects confessional literature: how can the spontaneity that says *I* merge with *me*, with a housetrained animal whose reactions are at once surprising and predictable, and which constantly slips through my fingers? Leiris refuses to be drawn into what that ambiguity implies: an endless series of attempts at self-understanding—a hopeless undertaking because the reworkings, denials and nuances eventually conceal everything important, rather than revealing it. He approaches himself as though he were an object, via a process of investigation, approximation and careful decoding, but keeps a respectful distance. His attitude is understanding and reserved. The combination of fascination and detachment obviously originates in, and is supported by, the character of the author himself.

Being the anthropologist of his personal institutions, Leiris encounters the same difficulties as any other anthropologist; the danger is that he will either alienate himself in the society he is studying or take as his sole point of reference the society from which he comes. These contradictory attitudes in fact result in the same misrecognition and the same surrender to the heady delights of exoticism. The anthropologist who wants so passionately to understand the meaning of, say, a religion forgets that it is a religion, or in other words a fantasmagoria, and, like Lévy-Bruhl invents a radically 'other' primitive mentality so as to avoid having to question his own certainties. Is there really no other way to understand the other? Do we have to choose between adopting his system for fear of betraying him, and contrasting it with our own supposedly categorical values, even though our devotion to them is not without an element of scorn? The anthropologist is basically reluctant either to convert or to be converted, and hesitates between abdication and proselytism.

We find this same feeling of unease in the man who, having travelled across a 'Phantom Africa' (Leiris 1934), resolves to take a fairly serious look at the society he is condemned never to leave: himself.

What is Leiris investigating? Who are his informants? They are rarely acts, decisions and their implications, or anything that a consciousness which believes itself to be sovereign inscribes in the course of things. They are dreams (the constant themes, not the playful shimmering of images), childhood memories (which reveal the origins, the force, of a mythology rather than decisive events), erotic experiences (which are not catalogued, but used to establish the obsessional backdrop) and his body (seen, not as a transmitter which is indifferent to its messages, but as the nucleus of a symbolism). In short, he seeks the meaning of his life in the *imaginary*. Thanks to his surrealist background, he can give the imaginary a real consistency. He also seeks the meaning of his life in the *meaning* that a taste, an obsessional fear or a fascinating allegory can both indicate and paralyse through its particularity and dispersal. It is this lost, opaque language, always on the point of disintegration, that Leiris is trying to introduce into the relative transparence of a methodical piece of writing. He peers into its workings and, like a linguist, subordinates etymology and history to current usage.

There is something of the inventory about *L'Age d'homme*. Let us look closely at our properties—which are unlikely to change now—carefully decipher this private symbolism, decode, analyse and cross check the schemata and anomalies of the speaking machine we call a person. Then what? Then we will be able to devote ourselves to other exercises.

Biffures was therefore not well received. He had to begin all over again. . . . People wondered what was wrong. This finicky reworking of what they had assumed to be a complete inventory was seen as an indication of a weakness typical of an author who, by his own admission, was quite incapable of seeing that his childhood was over and done with, of embracing life. And as the mood of times was warlike, it was said that this one, at least, would never reach manhood [*L'Âge d'homme*].

This strange reaction betrays a singular failure to recognize the nature of Leiris's undertaking. What was he attempting to do in *L'Age d'homme?* To objectify himself, but he did so quite openly and made no secret of it. Given that a discourse on the self is necessarily addressed to others, one may as well exploit the fact rather than mask it. Any confession is an ambiguous combination of things: Leiris refuses to be subjective, deliberately adopts the gaze of the other—an other who is familiar, but neither tender nor indulgent—and displaces the 'psychological' problem of sincerity on to the scientific problem of investigative techniques. He is not so much trying to capture a true image as to take an inventory of a collection of jumble.

Normally, one takes an inventory of a house when one moves in or out. Even though it is quite bare, a rented house—not one's own home—suddenly seems to contain a wealth of riches. You know what objects it contains, but would never think of counting them. But should you get the idea, and should it begin to obsess you in the way that it does Leiris, of taking an inventory of yourself, with the cold objectivity that allows a tenant to draw up an unemotional list of the very last doorknob without taking any particular interest in precious objects, you do not really know how to look at yourself. With a certain embarrassment. You can no longer invoke the mystery of your soul—everything has been laid out neatly for all to see—and dare not fall back on the ineffable—it's all been said, and just needs some reworking . . . Disoriented, in the way that I fell disoriented as I wander, somewhat distraught, through a strange town, or when I feel ill at ease in borrowed clothes that are not easily forgotten. Decentered, rather.

In Wertheimer's well known experiment (cited and discussed by Merleau-Ponty [1945, 248–50]) a subject looks at the room in which he is standing in an inclined mirror, without taking his eyes off it. Initially, he sees the walls 'slantwise'. Anything that moves—a man, a piece of cardboard falling to the floor—also seems to be falling obliquely. He finds the world 'queer', and experiences a sort of 'visual vertigo'. Suddenly, verticality is reestablished thanks to an instantaneous and systematic change, even though he has made no intellectual attempt to correct anything. The spatial level tilts. The subject 'feels he has the legs and arms he would need to walk and act in the reflected room; he inhabits the spectacle' (Merleau-Ponty 1945, 250).

Leiris attempts a similar experiment, but the outcome is very different. He looks at himself in a mirror but, unlike Narcissus, he does not lean forward to see himself in it. He tilts it. The point is that he is not seeking some impossible coincidence between image and self. He therefore tilts the mirror and turns it, as though someone standing by his side were holding it. He looks at himself in the mirror slantwise, from one side. But he cannot 'take up residence' in the system of ploys and habits he sees appearing before him, before us: it is the result of a piece of montage and not an ultimate truth.

In others words and unlike Wertheimer's subject, Leiris is not trying to tilt the spatial level and overcome vertigo. He keeps his distance from the slantwise individual he inventorizes or describes in *L'Age d'homme*. When he does become the individual who fascinates him, or makes that individual the site of his obsessions and fears, even the centre of his desires, he makes it clear, if only through the stark rigour of his style, that he is never completely absorbed into him. There is always a gap between them. That gap reveals what Sartre (1936, 81,82) calls the 'practical function' of the Ego: 'It is as though consciousness constituted the Ego as a false representation of itself, as though it were hypnotized by the Ego it has constituted, as though it made it its safeguard and its law.'[1]

No work has shown more clearly than *L'Age d'homme*—and it is this that gives it its decisive originality—that the ego is a psychical object that must—but never can—be 'reduced'. Unlike the literary hacks who, with a puerile mixture of excitement and bad faith, believe themselves to be what they are writing, Leiris springs the trap, even as he is describing the dreams he has about himself. By describing himself as he would a mythology, he discovers that his own ego is the root of this mythology, of a myth in which he refuses to be alienated. For him, decentering is not the by-product of an experiment. Decentering is what creates man: it is the primal rule of the game. Leiris's work is dedicated to an attempt to follow the implications of this rule. If the ego is an object, a correlate of all objects, and if it constitutes an imaginary unity which 'masks the spontaneity of consciousness' (Sartre 1936, 81), how are we to reveal the said subject?

Biffures provides a preliminary answer. Its intentions are obvious: 'If only I could have a clear understanding—after all these *bifurs* [bifurcations: 'forks', 'branching off'] (or attempt to explore all directions) and after so many *biffures* ['erasures'] (or successive eliminations of illusory values)—of what I want deep inside me' (Leiris 1948, 262).

---

1. This text might be compared with Lacan's ideas about the imaginary function of the ego. For Lacan (1949, 2), the ego is not a 'part-I', but a speculary image, 'the symbolic matrix in which the *I* is precipitated in a primal form.'

In his search for this misrecognized, basic desire, Leiris enters a dense, poor, shifty and disorganized world of imperfect, fleeting significations, and seems to get lost there. The method tries to imitate that of psychoanalysis: free association around emblematic images, encysted memories and words that are misunderstood or mispronounced, but although it is 'free' it is also very restrictive in that it rules out choice and system.[2] The tiresome repetitions are a working through of the intention that is both masked and betrayed in the themes that have been revealed.[3] The 'capricious point to point' (260) and the 'wanderings off the beaten track' trace the discontinuous progress of a word that constitutes his truth. This is indeed the heritage of Freud, who pursued meaning in its distortions—puzzle pictures and wordplay in dreams—the subject in marginal actions—bungled actions and slips of the tongue—and the unconscious in its roundabout expressions.

We can now understand why the voice that speaks to us in *Biffures* has lost the somewhat starchy self-assurance of *L'Age d'homme*. It alternates between the certainty that it has at last said all it had to say, and panic at the thought of the void: what difference is there between speech condemned to listen to itself in perpetuity, and silence?[4] The more Leiris speaks, the more he comes to resemble the man who went into exile in order to *forget*. Forget what? He has forgotten. Hence the endless cycle of discouragement ('The book I am now writing will be no more than a wooly rehash of *L'Age d'homme* with more padding' [Leiris 1948, 250] . . . 'I am bogged down in the task of splicing together notes' [64], and so on) and resolve ('To be set on what I really want'), which has less to do with personal quirks than with the rigour of the undertaking.

'I am spinning like a compass that has gone mad', he writes. Yet there is a direction to his search, and he can use language to steer by: 'the arachnid tissue of my relations with others transcends me, spreading its mysterious antenna in every direction' (Leiris 1948, 12). Leiris, a lonely prospector tunnelling through seams of words, is therefore

2. *L'Age d'homme* employed some psychoanalytic insights, but the method—a balance sheet rather than an exploration—was quite different.

3. Leiris speaks (1948, 76) of his *work [travail]* 'in the full sense of the term which, as Bréal notes in his essay on semantics (Bréal 1899), is etymologically connected with the idea of *cheval entravé* ['a hobbled horse'].

4. Chatter, 'a verbose way of churning oneself up' (Leiris 1948, 268), is no better than taciturnity. Keeping one's lip sealed is no better than soliloquising.

sometimes convinced that he is about to strike pure ore, the master word, and sometimes disenchanted: 'I always catch the shadow, not the substance.' The problem is that, when he approaches language, he is unable completely to abandon his belief in its omnipotence; he expects it to provide the revelation that learning to read may once have provided. Yet just when we think he has fallen victim to the illusion of an absolute-language, or even the delusion of basic language, he admits: 'The letters and words have obediently fallen into line, and what were once cabalistic sources of illumination have become—or almost become—dead letters' (71) and concludes, categorically, that 'Language is not, no matter how much we want it to be, a coded message sent to us by the ambassador to a distant absolute.'

Yet he never resigns himself to the fact; how could he when language 'sprawls out before him in its sheer, immense nudity'? He at first believes that this wall will send back an echo of all that exists, and of his own life. And he is not entirely wrong. As it is only because it is 'diacritical' (different from other signs) that a sign has a meaning, it is difficult to see how one can escape language, when one has eyes for nothing else. The world as 'little reality' (Breton 1924), but the reality of language is excessive, and it sometimes condemns anyone who manipulates words and sentences to silence, or at least paralyses him and petrifies him with terror.

This absolute respect for the signifier, which appears to have become a repository for the whole world, leads to madness. As the writings of people suffering from delusions show, madness begins, not with incoherence or absurdity, but with closure: communication is no longer possible, or desired, because that which creates meaning is simply there, as though it were frozen, and no longer refers to anything but itself. Leiris discovers that the language he regarded as an absolute is a 'simulacrum', and not the ideal terrain for the inscription of places and formulae.

Despite this intermittent fascination with language, there is still one other certainty, and it lies at the origins of *Biffures:* articulated language completes and recuperates a living expression that is lost 'in the gland and mucous membranes', to borrow Valéry's somewhat dismissive comment. The speaking subject is the whole subject. He can recapture and master the meaning that his actions both express and misrecognize. The work of speech thus merges with literature. The literary work ceases to be a double, and is bound to life by a word to word connection.

The fact remains that *Biffures* ends with an admission of failure. Leiris saw it as a refuge rather than a prospecting trip. Did he have any alternative? Can a 'self-analysis' ever end in a discovery, even if we are careful to formulate everything clearly, to use the most effective means? Imprisoned in a monologue, Leiris waits in vain for an answer; because he is fully preoccupied with closely watching a negative of himself, he ends up not knowing what he is saying, what he wants to say, or what he wants to hear himself say. Who is speaking through his mouth? And to whom?

'I stop, like a locomotive which finds that the way ahead is blocked and comes to a halt in the middle of nowhere after having given a volley of whistle-blasts' (Leiris 1948, p. 278). Then the track is clear again. What has given Leiris this new impetus? How did he escape the private symbolism he tried in vain to decipher (by trying to decipher it, he blocked his own intention of 'building myself a sort of system which is valid in terms of the norm, and not only for me' [270]; language betrayed the demand for universality implicit within it, and became a soliloquy). It is *Fourbis* (Leiris 1955), the next stage in the 'point to point', that provides the answer.

Here we have a man who thought he had been thrown into a dungeon for life, when, like certain figures in Bosch, he was in fact shutting himself up inside a glass bubble. The passwords that should set him free keep him captive, as though he himself were blowing the bubble. The more he speaks, the more he seems to condemn himself to hear only his own voice. When he tries to use cryptology to decipher reality, he finds only his own symbols, and turns up what is in fact the very reason for his emotions: the rule of the game [*règle du jeu*] (which is also the rule of the 'I' [*je*]). What is he doing in his circular dungeon? Walking up and down, back and forth, repeating himself, getting bored; pointless tribulations, a slow song which merges into the silence, the same old song, the same old tune, chains of words that make only a little noise.

There is nothing accidental about the clear admission of defeat at the end of *Biffures*—he has to break off at some point. It means that, having reached the point in his research, Leiris knows that he is at an impasse. If he can do no more than splice notes together, he may as well give up; when a beaten man admits defeat, isn't he admitting the truth about himself?

Now that the whole man has been reduced to a word, it is in his very style that we see the shadow projected by the crystaline walls which imprison him as we read him; the falterings, questions and parentheses are simply a hugely magnified version of the questions, falterings and parentheses that make up Leiris himself.

Yet *Fourbis* (Leiris 1955), which reopens the cycle,is not simply a return to an uninterrupted piece of research. It is, rather, a new beginning: with the very first words we sense that the voice has changed. In *L'Age d'homme*, we were walking through a private museum, learning the grammar and elementary syntax of a language that we were later able to see at work (in *Biffures*). Any language that is spoken is halting and incomplete when compared with the image we have of it. What had once been resolutely asserted had to be struck out [*biffer*], not in order to complete the portrait, and still less to attempt another, but simply to reveal, beyond all these gaps [*biffures*] and deviations [*bifurs*] a subject that no behaviour and no consciousness will consent to reveal to us. *Biffures*, then, was the negative of *L'Age d'homme*. As the title indicates, *Fourbis* [clobber] announces a new reversal.

The book opens with a meditation on death, whose role is now to restart the point to point. Yet death has never been absent from Leiris's work, all of which is placed under the sign of an obsession with death. The obsession is visible in every line, either because Leiris admits to it or because it finds immediate expression (especially in anything to do with mineralization). It is also visible in the ego structure it implies (the ego is a fortress; others are aggressors), in the play of phantasies in *Aurora* (Leiris 1928) and in the symptoms that are literally presented category by category in *L'Age d'homme*: 'women of classical antiquity' (1939, 61–62), 'Lucretia and Judith' (1939, 157–80), and so on. The obsession is not parasitic; Leiris's undertaking is rooted in it. There in fact exists a form of self-consciousness which is synonymous with consciousness of death, death being the negation of particularity on merely the institution of a nameless universality. It is probably in the fantasmagoric discourse of *Aurora* that we see most clearly that death and the ego are two sides of a single obsession. 'The death of the world equals the death of myself (Leiris 1928, 40) . . . Death hung over me day and night, like a dull threat (840 . . . Fearing death, I hated life (because death is life's crowning achievement)' (400).

Death is already present in its purest signification: neither a fatal reckoning nor a cause for worry, but a negation of all particularity, a pure limit against which the human subjet must of course be tested. 'And so I come to cathedral Death, to the third person singular I just

erased [*biffais*] with a stroke of the pen. Death, a grammatical bifurcation which subjects the world and myself to its ineluctable syntax, a
rule which makes all discourse a wretched mirage that covers up the
nothingness of objects, no matter what words I pronounce, no matter
what *I* I profer' (Leiris 1927, 40–41).

Once he has recognized this he/it of death, Leiris can easily admit:
'I always find it more painful than most people to express myself other
than by means of the pronoun 'I', not that this should be seen as a
particular sign of my pride; it is simply that, for me, the word 'I' sums
up the structure of the world' (39). Even so, he is not writing his own
confession, but that of Siriel, his inverted *double*. His double wanders
in a state of white *mourning*, wearing 'in a breastplate similar to the
breastplate that could have been forged from his skeleton, had it suddenly been externalized. His double both provides a defence against
death (as we can see from so many primitive beliefs) and ensures that
we can master death.'[5]

Aurora is the very emblem of narcissism. It could have no better
seal than this alliance between the ego, death and the double, as the ego
can avoid the vertigo of death—the vertigo of the ego itself—only
through a phantasy relation with the other to whom it delegates both
its obsessional features and a certain power that must save it from the
sickness unto death and its fragmenting effects.[6] The problem is that
Leiris is too lucid to be enchanted with this phantasmogoria, which he
seems to denounce even as he surrenders to it. This is why this surrealist text is so astonishing: its density is being eroded, its flight into
the imaginary curbed, and its shimmering is unattractively lustreless.

If we do not wish to surrender to vertigo, to a vertiginous object,
flight is our only escape. Rupture, liquidation, departure. The psychoanalysis Leiris began after *Aurora* (and about which he remains very
discreet) must have been undertaken as a result of a resolve to abandon
everything and, first of all, to destroy the ego, to escape both its mirages
and the fascination with death. Likewise the African trip, which
proved to be an encounter with phantoms rather than the advent of a
truth; in Africa, Leiris made the bitter discovery that he was 'a purely
spatial nomad who dragged behind him his worries and manias—

5. We cannot experience death as an event; we can only experience its equiv-
alents: 'When we copulate, we at least know what happens afterwards, and we can be
witnesses, and bitter witnesses at that, to the subsequent disaster.'
6. 'In truth they were neither men nor women, but quite literally and quite
simply fragments of bodies' (Leiris 1928 32).

which were made worse, rather than better, by his relative isolation. Any attempt to make a radical break feeds on an impossible desire to be dead and to be aware of the fact. In the imaginary, the contradiction can be resolved by the myth of the double. It is this contradiction that makes the *idea* of suicide so fascinating (not actual suicide, as there is no such thing as a privileged death). In order to make a real break, one must be in possession of a truth that makes it possible to denounce masks, pretences and reflections; otherwise it is merely another form of flight, a double mirage.

In *L'Age d'homme*, Leiris therefore approaches his own death obliquely, after a failed break, a failed 'suicide' attempt. Refusing to play on the ambiguities of narcissistic passion, which are also those of literature, and at the same time taking care to avoid their traps, Leiris, as we have seen, follows through the implications of defining the ego as an alter ego, and 'suicides', so to speak, the ego by constituting it and interpreting it as an other. As Blanchot (1949) notes, it is a 'gaze from beyond the tomb' that Leiris turns on himself. This gaze is much more pitiless than that of any concrete other—the other is always both accomplice and traitor—and, because it is impossible to challenge, it puts you in the position of being guilty.[7] How can one not admit that *I* am what *he* thinks of me? This encounter between an objectivized ego and the 'third-person' dimension—death—against which Leiris tests himself should create the possibility of a 'first-person' I, hitherto misrecognized, perverted or simply distorted by daily life, which can at last begin to speak.

'I am lying in my bed, exactly as I should be in reality, but with my forehead pressed against the dusty white-washed side of a large cylinder, a sort of cistern, which is little taller than I am, and which is none other than myself, made real and externalized' (Leiris 1961, 60).

'A sign is being placed on a grave (mine?) as an epitaph; it sums up the life of the deceased in a few lines. It is entitled "argument" ' (Leiris 1961, 150).

'I put my head into an orifice rather like a bullseye window looking on to a dark, enclosed space, as though I wanted to look inside. . . . My anxiety is due to the fact that, as I lean out over this walled space and look into its inner darkness, I am looking into myself' (Leiris 1961).

These three dreams—the ego made real, a life already lived (on

---

7. 'I always behaved like an accursed man who wanted nothing so much as to take this cure to extremes.'

another occasion, Leiris dreams that he buys a booklet in which he reads all that lies in store for him; his future is already a future interior), anxiety unto death—articulate the whole of Leiris's relationship with death, the relationship that underlies *L'Age d'homme* which, although it is described in the preface as 'a risk run' (Leiris 1945–46, 16–17), seems rather to be an attempt at exorcism. Just as the double (in this case, the mythological ego) is destroyed by the pitiless inventory that has been taken of it, so his confession frees him from the unease of a confused existence: by tearing off his masks and denouncing story-telling, he can exorcise his anxiety about being nothing.[8]

Leiris could not paint a more truthful portrait than that given in *L'Age d'homme*—there is no such thing as a true ego, merely a man who measures himself by the standard of the true; he had yet to find the path that would give that man the means to speak, to constitute his truth by adopting a systematic, but not pre-ordained, approach or, in short, by moving from the book-as-product to the book-as-speech. That book was *Biffures*.

At this stage, death should no longer be present. And death is not present, or at least not in the form of an obsession. Once the ego has been reduced, the vertigo of death fades, the strange thing being that the subject had to be both subjected to death and preserved from its threats. Yet whilst death is no longer directly perceptible in *Biffures*, its shadow is still projected in the form of stagnation and it is perceptible in the very words themselves. Leiris does not conceal the fact. How could he?

In *Aurora* ('imaginary diamonds on an imaginary mirror' [Leiris 1928, 87–8]), he showed that he had no illusions about the false hardness of all words, or about the poverty and bombast of a poet dragging with him 'a sabre of badly sharpened phrases which can cut only a chamfered void, and not the heads I would like to collect in my basket' (40).

Biffures reveals the misfortunes and ridiculous ways of a prose writer who is perpetually at odds with his life, a text which can sometimes be put into a couple of words and which is sometimes torn

8. Leiris recognizes, of course, that Freudianism 'offers everyone a convenient way of acquiring a tragic status by seeing himself as a new Oedipus' and notes elsewhere that his memory has a natural tendency to retain 'anything that can serve as the basis for a mythology.'

completely asunder. To take only one of a thousand admissions: I am forced to admit that—like someone who really does collect plants—all that I can apprehend is no more use than a dried stem, a flower on the point of crumbling into dust' (Leiris 1948, 241–42). One thinks of Freud's observations to the effect that, whereas everything conscious becomes worn away, the unconscious is indestructible. Yet if the unconscious is set free, perhaps it too crumbles into dust. Leiris does not capture the origins and avatars of his truth; he captures, at best, a few artificially linked fragments of his legend, 'poor phantoms of realities that are always behind me and already circulating amongst the ruins even as I write' (242).

It seems that, whatever the methods and the stages of his approach, the only game Leiris can play is one involving a shadow, which may never have been a substance, whose only rule is the rule of an impersonal and therefore neutralized death which still petrifies him, authorizes him to grow old (one begins to understand his obsessive fear of aging) but not to develop a history and pick up his baggage (whether or not he is happy about it is a different story).

Why the stagnation? What is the significance of the interrogative, problematic and starchy character of this text? Why is he so hesitant, and what about? It is all the more difficult to understand in that, unlike Proust's, Leiris's search is profoundly 'interested' (at least to begin with; as it progresses, it peters out of its own accord). Now, Proust never gives this feeling of sterility; the temporality of his project implies metamorphosis as well as degradation. in Leiris, on the other hand, nothing seems to move. For him, of course, acting is a way of speaking, but by now he is reading himself rather than speaking.

In order to understand this stagnation, this absence of history, we have to relate it to its *raison d'être:* the obstinacy, the curious insistence that makes Leiris retrace the same paths, fit together and take apart the same memories again and again, regardless of his dejection.

Leiris is not looking for a secret that might be tracked down by painstaking investigation (judging by his earliest writings, no one ever went around an estate with such care, or at such an early age). The 'marches and countermarches, the diversions, the retraced steps and the standstills', the tormented repetitions and the sterile debates are no more than the mark of a desire—anxious because it is powerless to obtain the wherewithal for its fulfilment—to escape the 'circular dungeon'."

In *Fourbis*, death, hitherto the categorical rule of Leiris's universe, seems at last to find a new function. It ceases to be a pure, impersonal gaze which transmutes everything it touches into minerals or steel, and which forces man—a terrified, defeated and petrified man—to be nothing more than a shrunken ego. It finally consents to being tamed and provides Leiris with an opening on to both himself and the world, as though another totality, an absolute other, were possible, and not merely the dazzling totality and other represented by moments when all antinomies miraculously fuse. Rather than existing outside time, in *Fourbis*, these privileged instants are captured by a form of speech which suddenly finds a more generous rhythm wherein *I* and *he* can finally merge into a single voice.

This new approach, which we can see in the working through of a few experiences that makes up the first chapter of the book, does not allow him to transcend death (no consciousness of death has the ability to transcend it), but it does allow him to recognize that death has a positive value: it is now inscribed under a different sign. In *Fourbis*, we see the beginnings of this rotary movement. Until now, outwitting death actually meant submitting to its rule, either by mimetically adopting an appropriate form of being or playing dead—both at the objective level of dress and the subjective level of writing—or by seeking an illusory mastery (an interest in egotism, in the corrida). Here, as the rule finally merges with the search for the rule and with the book itself, Leiris anticipates death in a very different way: he outlines the totalizing movement that defines death, articulates in a simple decree the law that ends in death and sums up death. *Making death real* is the only way to defeat death.

This new stance alters Leiris's perspective considerably: this is the subject matter of *Fourbis* and it would be pointless to add a commentary. 'The ever-so slight events that shine forth here and there in our lives' are no longer 'places where the world and the self are tangential', and they no longer deserve an almost religious devotion. Like certain dreams, they merely condense a set of intentions that still have to be brought into the real circuit of existence. Although he is no longer 'fooled by a sort of ritual mimicry, by simulacra of positive actions', Leiris has not therefore abandoned his mythology as a result of some positivist enlightenment; he decathects it, and tries to fulfil the singular wish from which it originated in his work rather than in pantasies. Language loses its oracular value and becomes a medium for the articulation and determination of the truth. Leiris can now escape the tormenting dilemma of either magical change or perpetual stagnation.

Having said that, Leiris's *oeuvre* is still an endless encounter with the self; he is completely committed to a dialectic of recognition, to a search for an object whose 'absence explains why life is spent in a state of anxiety and idleness', and nostalgia for 'a destiny which, retrospectively, makes it worthy of being loved'. He defines himself as a man whose nostalgia 'leaves things far behind so as to retain a desire for them, or so as to regret them'. He still believes that 'a slender thread means that one can be in contact with oneself.' In a word, he cannot tear himself away from himself, is still threatened by the gaze of others, and by the absolute other known as death, and knows some respite only when he believes himself to be 'seen completely, but spared the intrusion of the gaze' (and this lack of reciprocity removes him from the human debate). He knows that he is totally dependent upon objects, and therefore distances himself from them all the more. He knows that he is condemned to an existence whose limited nature has not escaped him.

Those who are in love with life say with impatience that he should let himself go. Our man simply refused to listen. He is still deciphering the same facts, examining the same myths, ('prisms of intimate crumbs' [Leiris 1939, 99]), spelling out the same glossary, the same neurosis [*névrose*], if you insist, still stripping the petals from 'the vain rose of the brain' [*rose vaine du cerveau*] (100), facing up to the same anxiety, the same 'sticky shed, teeming with devices that can strangle' [*hangar poisseux, foisonnant de cent engins pour étrangler*] (74), suffering, exorcising and taming the same death, that minotaur who likes men, that over-salty traumatism' [*minotaure amateur d'hommes, saumâtre traumatisme*]' (99). His insistence on doing so may be strange, but we would do better to understand the reasons for it than to contrast it with the so-called certainties of what we somewhat hastily, and with less humour and prudence than Leiris, call manhood.

It is true that literature is not the only way of testing oneself against death. It is not quite so certain that there is any literature which is not nourished by an existence dedicated to speaking its name, to situating itself, to recognizing its one desire in all its mediations, its shining object amid the dullness of the tasks that occupy it. It cannot be denied that there are other ways of living one's freedom. Yet how can we criticise Leiris for having chosen this way? We should, rather, be admiring the unparalleled honesty with which he pursues his task and his refusal to reduce the antinomies between life and death, myth and reality, work and speech, literary language and day to day prose. It is that which gives his writing its incomparable tension.

—Translated by David Macey

EMMANUEL LÉVINAS

Transcending Words: Concerning Word-Erasing*

The Surrealist project goes beyond the claims of a literary school. Its purpose is to identify metaphysical freedom and poetic freedom. The whimsical fantasy of the dream-work, in its very absurdity, does not evolve out of a fatalistic thwarting of human dignity but maneuvers according to a process of emancipation. The dream is not a privilege bestowed by genius. The non-sensical is the most commonly shared thing there is. Yet, Breton's first manifesto displayed, on the one hand, a naive confidence in the clandestine and miraculous forces at work in the Unconscious. His references concerning Freud still read like allusions to some mythological realm ripe with promises of hidden treasures. On the other hand, his critique of the conscious mechanisms of thought did not so much proceed out of their analysis as out of his following them into the dead-end prospects where their use eventually led.

Michel Leiris who belonged for a while to the Surrealist group also extolled in his last book—albeit in his own way—the great power of the dream-work. Only instead of positing some would-be mystical power in the Unconscious, he finds actual causes to his dream. Reasons drawn from conscious life. At first glance, his images owe their richness and their seemingly unexpected quality to the *process of idea-association* of which Michel Leiris religiously describes the "latent birth."

Throughout the first half of the book, the reader witnesses a prodigious amplifying movement of Rimbaud's famous sonnet. Only the

---

*This article, "La Transcendance des mots," first appeared in *Les Temps modernes*, no. 44 (1949); 1090–95.

YFS 81, *On Leiris,* ed. Blanchard, © 1992 by Yale University.

suggested correspondences are no longer mysterious. They are narrated through their genesis. Michel Leiris deals more in word chemistry than in verbal alchemy. From page 128 on, that chemistry is applied to facts, situations, memories. It properly becomes the narrative content, being both the work of art it puts forward and a reflection on the essence of that art; a process which is certainly linked to the tradition of French poetry from Mallarmé to Blanchot, a tradition in which the emotional impulse constituting the work content is the very same impulse behind the creation of that content.

In the very last part of his book, Michel Leiris reveals the process at work within his art: *bifurs* or word-erasing [*biffures*] which lends its title to the book as well as gives a meaning to the astonishing rehabilitation of word-association. *Bifurs*—for sensations, words and memories continually cut thought away from the direction toward which it seemingly steered and take it further into unsuspected paths; word-erasures [*biffures*]—for the univocal meaning in those elements is ceaselessly corrected and overinscribed. Yet the point of these *bifurs* or word-erasing is not so much about exploring the new paths thus opened, or even about pondering their corrected meaning, but rather about pinpointing thought at the rare moment when it sideslips into something other than itself. Only because of this basic ambiguity at the heart of the *bifur*, is the process of word-association made possible.

Whereas we are prone to reduce the signifying function to word-association and to think that the multiplicity of meaning produced by the verbal or other sign can be explained away by the network of associations where that verbal sign is located, instead with the notion of *bifur*, the process of word-association loses its fundamental role. Thought is originally word-erasing—that is to say, symbolic. And because thought is symbolic, ideas can hook up with one another and create a connecting network. Hence, whether this network is produced by the circumstances under which the word was learned or by its vocal similarities with other words, or even by its written form—thus enriched with everything the signs of writing themselves conjure up, this network owes its value not so much to the fact that it connects one thought to another but rather to the fact that it guarantees the presence of one given thought *within* another. Just as animals in fairy tales do not merely convey a moral lesson but, by their tangible presence, give richness to the idea suggested, thought, at the very time of its erasure, retains the validity of its erased meaning. The various meanings thus interact with one another. Surrealist freedom is not opposed to other thought mechanisms—it is, on the contrary, their overriding principle.

The process of word-association, once understood in the context of word-erasing becomes a system of thinking which stands beyond the classical categories of representation and identity. The overreaching of thought is indeed reminiscent of duration according to Bergson—although Bergson's conception turns this negation of identity into a representational process of becoming. The originality of word-erasing lies in its positing of multiplicity as simultaneous and conscience as irreducibly ambiguous. Michel Leiris's memories such as they are narrated according to his "rule of the game" does not give the impression—curiously enough—of a temporal scheme. Rather, the ambiguity of word-erasing creates a space.

A parallel between the process of word-erasing and the works of modern painters would prove to be interesting. There has been a recent exhibit of Charles Lapicque's paintings. By destroying perspective as the order of perceiving, approaching, and as the practical means of acceding to objects, Charles Lapicque creates a space which is above all the order of a simultaneity—process similar to a literary description leading into a tableau not by reproducing a continuous stretch but by putting together selected details into an order which is determined by the nature of those details and by their power of suggestion. Space as such does not accommodate things. Rather, things sketch out space from their erasure. In turn, the space in each object sheds volume. The line of ambiguity steps out from behind the line of fixity. Lines throw off their skeletal functioning in order to become the infinite process of a possible coming together. Shapes play variations on their essential themes similar to the ocean foam which Charles Lapicque is now working on and in which sensitive matter condenses into infinite suggestions ranging from one form to another. Variation on themes, yet not musical ones, for it knows nothing of duration; only simultaneous and spatial. On account of its being unique, the very form of a painting would stop the game of word-erasing. A Lapicque painting is accompanied by variations which do not act as *studies* leading toward the *ne varietur* end-version of the work, but which all stand on the same ground. Open-endedness, instead of completion, paradoxically appears to be the fundamental category of modern art.

However, doesn't the spatial quality in the play of word-erasing come from its visual aspect? The profusion of word-erasures is indeed the return of consciousness to sensory experience, the return of the sensory world to its own sensory essence, its aesthetic experience. Yet, again, isn't it true that the particular brand of symbolism imbedded in the aesthetic essence of reality owes its explanation to the very nature of visual experience under which Western civilization eventually subsumes any kind of spiritual life? The aesthetic essence deals with ideas, it is luminescent, it seeks clarity and evidence. It ends up in the unveiled world of phenomena. Everything is immanent to it.

Seeing means being in a self-sufficient world that is completely here. Any vision reaching beyond the realm of given facts remains within that realm. The infinity of space, just like the infinity of the signifier to which the sign refers, remains no less earthbound. Vision is a link to being in such a way that being once seen precisely appears as a world. Sounds in turn are given to intuition and can be given out. This is where the primacy of vision lies in relation to the other senses. And the universality of art also rests on that primacy of vision. It produces beauty in nature, it calms and soothes it. The arts, even those based on sound, produce silence.

A silence which can sometimes be in bad faith or weighty or frightful. We identify as the need for criticism that need which yearns to reach out to someone, in spite of and beyond the peaceful wholeness of beauty.

Sound—and conscience conceived as hearing—includes within itself the splitting apart of the always completed world of vision and art. Sound as a whole rings out, detonates, and is scandalous. Whereas, in the realm of vision, forms embrace and soothe their contents, sound is like the sensory world overflowing itself, forms being unable to hold their contents—the world ripping asunder—that by which *this* world *here* extends a dimension which cannot be converted into vision. In that sense, sound is the intrinsic symbolical function—the flight beyond the given. Yet, the reason it can still keep the appearance of a phenomenon, as *here*, is that its transcending function only holds sway in the verbal sound. The sound and rumor of nature are deceptive words. To truly hear a sound is to hear a vocable. Pure sound is the Word.

Philosophy and contemporary sociology have accustomed us to underestimating the direct social contact of people speaking, in order to favor silence or the complex relations determined by civilization and its categories, such as customs, law, and culture. A scornful bias against words which is the result of the pitfalls intrinsic to language—

its many faceted ability to turn into chatter and impediment. Such a scorn however cannot have the best of the situation whose privilege is granted to Robinson in the beauty of tropical landscape when, having broken no ties with civilization either by his tools, or his morals, or his calendar, he experiences the greatest event of his life on the island: the moment at last when a man, speaking, takes the place of the unspeakable sadness of echo.

This means that the other's actual presence does have its importance in social interaction. More importantly, however, it means that, far from expressing a pure and simple coexistence with the "I" or far from being justified by the romantic metaphor of "living presence," that presence is achieved through hearing and draws its meaning from the role, played by the spoken word, of a transcendental origin. It is because the word will not become incarnate that it achieves its presence among us. The presence of the Other is a teaching presence. That is why the word as teaching is more than the experience of the real, why also the master does more than mind midwifery. Indeed it tears the experience away from its aesthetic complacency, from its position *here* where it peacefully lies. It transforms it into a being by calling upon it. In this sense, we might have once said that criticism—as a living being speaking to another living being—brings back the image where art delights, to the genuinely real being. The language of criticism pulls us out of that dreaming which also harbors artistic language. Of course, in its written form, it continually calls for more criticism; books keep calling for more books. Yet the proliferation of the printed word stops or reaches its highest point when the living word comes into it, at the moment, again, when criticism blossoms into teaching.

The privilege which the living word, made the ear, has over the image-word or the already picturesque sign also appears when the act of speaking is considered.

For is speaking only putting words into signs as the writings suggest? Disfigured words, *"paroles gelées"* [frozen words] where language is already turned into documents and vestiges. The living word fights against thought turning into remains, it fights against words coming out when there is no one to listen to them. Oral expression entails the impossibility of being in itself, of keeping its thought to itself. It consequently involves a lack in the position of the subject in which the "I" enjoys a given world. Speaking means interrupting my existence as both subject and master, yet without exposing me since it leaves me as simultaneously subject and object. My voice brings the context in which that dialectical configuration is concretely carried out. The speaking subject does not set up the world in relation to him/herself and does not position him/herself just simply in the midst of his/her self-representation as does the artist; the speaking subject does it in relation to the Other. This privilege of the Other can be understood as soon as we admit that the foremost fact of life is neither the *in-itself* nor the *for-itself* but the *"pour l'autre"* [*for the other*]; or, again, as soon as human existence becomes being. Through the spoken word, the subject who posits himself also exposes himself and, in a sense, prays.

According to the foregoing comments, indeed too cursory for so serious a subject, the very moment of expression becomes located outside of its traditional subordination to thought. The common idea according to which words are only good for communicating—or concealing—thought, relies on such an ancient and venerable tradition that no one dares challenge it. It is our supposition that Michel Leiris's word-erasing magnificently exhausts all the possibilities of developing and furthering thinking thought when the latter touches upon the sensory matter that molds words. Yet, those possibilities still rely on the privilege given to thought as it is expressed in the age-old language of "whatever can be properly thought out" ("Ce qui se conçoit bien . . . ").* For Michel Leiris, in the final analysis, the wealth brought out by language can be measured only by its counterpart in thought content.

—Translated by Didier Maleuvre

---

*Probable reference to the French saying: "Ce qui se conçoit bien s'énonce bien" [Whatever can be properly thought out can also be properly spoken].—Translator's note.

MAURICE BLANCHOT

Glances from Beyond the Grave*

Michel Leiris has preceded the new edition of *Manhood* with an essay in the form of a preface which constitutes the most cogent commentary on this work and renders the others useless. In this essay, entitled "The Autobiographer as *Torero*,"[1] he illuminates perfectly the intentions to which we owe this book, one of the central works of so-called modern literature. What did he want in wanting to write it? First, he wanted to escape the gratuitousness of literary works and to accomplish a real act, threatening for its author and capable of signifying the same peril for him that "the bull's sharp horn" represents in other games. Beyond this, he wanted to accomplish a work that might shed some light upon himself, for his own benefit and for others, while simultaneously freeing him from certain obsessions and allowing him to attain a true "vital fulfillment." Finally, he wanted to write a book which would be dangerous for his other books and for literature in general, showing "the other side of the deck," making visible "in all of their unenthralling nakedness, the realities which formed the more or less disguised warp, beneath the shining appearance" of his other writings (*L'Age d'homme*, 15, [157], translation slightly altered).

All of these intentions respond to problems from which literature cannot be separated. Writing is nothing if it does not lead the writer

---

*This passage is taken from Maurice Blanchot, *La Part du feu* (Paris: Gallimard, 1949). With the permission of Gallimard.

1. "De la Littérature comme une Tauromachie" in Michel Leiris, *L'Age d'homme* (Paris: Gallimard, 1939), 9–24. The English translations here are from *Manhood* trans. Richard Howard, (New York, North Point, 1984), 153–64. All references to citations have been provided by the translator. English translations will be indicated in the text by brackets. —Translator's note.

YFS 81, *On Leiris*, ed. Blanchard, © 1992 by Yale University.

into a hazardous movement that will change him in one way or the other. Writing is only a worthless game if this game does not become an adventurous experience, in which he who undertakes it, engaging himself on a road whose destination eludes him, can learn what he does not know and lose what prevents him from knowing. And then, to write, yes; but if writing always makes the act of writing more difficult, tends to draw him away from the fluency that words continually receive at the hands of those who are most skillful at it.

Manhood is not an autobiography, nor is it simple confessions; it has even less to do with Memoires. Autobiography is the work of a living, vital memory, which wants and is able to recapture time in its very movement. Autobiography's principal merit, outside of its content, lies in its rhythm, its effusiveness, which is not a synonym for a confidence but rather evokes the power of the waves, the truth of something which flows, expands and only takes form in a flux. *Henri Brulard, Souvenirs d'égotisme,* Quincey sometimes, and the second part of *Si le grain ne meurt* are the models of this history which finds its self, not as already made and solidified history, but as existence turned towards the future and which, at the moment of its recounting, seems always in the making and unknown to the very person who narrates in the past tense. As for Memoires, we know about those: deliberate and methodical reconstitutions, works of reflection, sometimes on art and science. Existence here (even if it is a private existence) is history because it is historical. It presents itself as always having been, with all the dignity and solemnity due to the monumental presence of a past over which the author himself has ceased to have any claim. The *Mémoires d'outre-tombe* have this exemplary virtue: they rise from the grave, says M. Maurice Levaillant, and Chateaubriand, with his incomparable sense of the past, confirms this in terms one cannot smile about: "I was pressed to present parts of these *Mémoires* during my lifetime; I prefer to speak from the bottom of my coffin; my narrative will thus be accompanied by these voices which have something sacred about them, because they come from the sepulcher."[2] But, if the truth be told, it is not death which speaks in these *Mémoires,* but rather existence as dead, as always having been,

2. I am translating Blanchot's own altered version of the original citation from the "Préface Testamentaire" of *Mémoires d'outre-tombe,* vol. I (Paris: Flammarion, 1961, 1982), 6. *The Memoires of Chateaubriand,* selected, translated and with an introduction by Robert Baldick (New York: Alfred A. Knopf, 1961), xxii.

always also a thing of the past immobilized in a life which remains, in its grandiose manner, alien to any future and even to the future of death.

Manhood approaches Confessions. As in Confessions, its author wants to "reveal himself," to "admit publicly to certain shameful deficiencies or cowardices of which he is most ashamed" (*L'Age d'homme*, 10, [154]). The object of Confessions is to make public that which is only private, and to do this with a moral or at least a practical intention. One confesses, first of all, to bring to light what is hidden, then to make the day judge of this hidden depth, and finally to unload this occulted life onto the day. Michel Leiris has told us in his preface: "By means of an autobiography dealing with a domain in which discretion is *de rigueur*. . . . I intended to rid myself for good of certain embarrassing images, at the same time that I revealed my features with the maximum of clarity as much for my own use as to dissipate any erroneous sense of myself which others might have had" (*L'Age d'homme*, 12, [155–56]). And then he speaks of *catharsis*, of deliverance, of a discipline which comes along to complete the first results of a psychoanalytic cure. Perhaps there is here a fairly obscure intention in the book. One could observe that this intention contradicts the others, that if the author writes to free himself from dangerous obsessions, this "good" he expects from his book greatly diminishes its threatening character. If, by dint of sincerity, he expects to cure himself of "certain deficiencies and instances of cowardice," at the same time he will certainly be able to experience all the dangers of this sincerity by making relations with certain people who are close to him more difficult. But in the end, it will only be an evil which anticipates a good, a momentary inconvenience which he accepts in order to rid himself of some far more serious ones, a risk he takes in order to live thereafter free from the risks to which his obsessions and deficiencies expose him.

One could further note that confession presupposes a strange entanglement of motives and effects. Certainly, calling oneself a coward is not easy. But, precisely, this does not go without courage, and the witness of confession runs the risk of noticing above all, beneath the cowardice, the courageous resoluteness which confesses, and he will see this all the more clearly if the confession is forthright, rigorous and precise. If, furthermore, the person who owns up to deficiencies is counting on this confession to free himself from them—if, by confessing that he is a coward, he finds himself, after this confession, to be the most courageous of men—one can see how this maneuver turns out in the end to his advantage and is likely to reward the person who attempts it for its risks.

The author of *Manhood* not only is not unaware of these difficulties but he also denounces them, or at least he denounces other equivalent ones. The latter ones first: the problem is that the danger of exposing the self in writing is rarely mortal. The bull's horn which threatens the writer is only the shadow of a horn. The scandal may be great, but literature is that sword which heals the one it wounds: the esthetic value of the scandal, its beauty, soon transform it, and the book for which one had braved scorn ultimately brings admiration and glory. Cheating thus lies at the beginning of every literary enterprise like a tragedy. But there is something more serious: "What I did not realize was that at the source of all introspection is a predilection for self-contemplation, and that every confession contains a desire to be absolved" (*L'Age d'homme*, 13, [156]). In fact, this predilection and this pleasure are the only immediate "benefits" confession reserves for whomever abandons himself to it: the other advantages we pointed out remain very ambiguous. To paint ourselves as we are, that is to say, more mediocre than we wanted to appear and others think we are, (though this confession may promise us considerable consolation for later), at the moment that this is done, only the grief and difficulty in doing it count—he who confesses to cowardice sees the cowardice he declares rather than the courage of his confession, and the book where this confession is inscribed is still only a stuttering sketch, completely unaware of its destiny to become the successful, praised, and admired book. The confession is thus certainly a risk; a remedy, though perhaps an illusory one, which, far from making obscure things disappear, renders them more obscure, more obsessive, and will precipitate the failure it was supposed to prevent.

"To consider myself objectively was still to consider myself—to keep my eyes fixed on myself instead of turning them beyond and transcending myself in the direction of something more broadly human" (*L'Age d'homme*, 13–14, [156]). On this level, confession is indeed secretly undermined by the different kinds of satisfaction it brings. Some take pride in their humiliation and pleasure in their humiliating confidences: this is sometimes the case of Rousseau. But the pleasure can be of a more subtle and more formidable order. One can thus find contentment in looking at oneself without contentment, one finds a cloudy voluptuousness in clearing everything up, and rigor becomes weakness. The more one is frank, the more frankness will satisfy the duplicity at the bottom of one's heart. The more demanding one is of the self, the more this exactitude will be the source of dangerous faults. There is a sin in confession which no confession can overcome, because it is committed in its confession and is aggravated by absolution: the fault here is linked to justification, to innocence, and yet to want this innocence is necessary, nor can one do without it, so that everything is a fault, both the confession and the refusal of it. Such is essentially the category of the demoniacal of which Kierkegaard spoke.

Michel Leiris chose the fault of confession, and this is doubtlessly a *felix culpa* since we owe to it a book which has become a classic today. But, we must further observe that willingness is the opposite of complacency here, that it not only does not signify an excessive inclination to speak but, rather, it originates in the refusal to say anything at all, in an "I cannot speak" which ends up forcing him to speak by its very excess. "All my friends know it: I am an addict of confession; yet what impels me—especially with women—to such confidences is timidity. When I am alone with a person whose sex alone makes her so different from me, my feeling of isolation and misery becomes so great that, despairing of finding anything conversational to say to my interlocutor, incapable too of courting her should I happen to desire her, I begin—for lack of any other subject—to speak of myself. As my phrases flow the tension rises, and I come to the point of establishing, between my partner and myself, a strange dramatic current. For, the more my present uneasiness disturbs me, the more I speak of myself desperately, emphasizing my sense of solitude and of separation from the world, until I am ultimately uncertain whether this tragedy I have described corresponds to the permanent reality of my being or is only the imagined expression of this momentary anguish which I suffer as soon as I come into contact with another person and am somehow called upon to speak" (*L'Age d'homme*, 157–58, [105–06]).

We can see that what gives birth to the most profound speech is the vertigo arising from the impossibility of speaking, and how the motive and the sole theme of this speech is its own impossibility: it speaks to itself as though it were not speaking, and because of this, it is limitless, nothing can interrupt it since it has no content to exhaust,—nothing, except that at a certain moment it discovers itself speaking, speaking endlessly and therefore, conscious of its deception, it reverts to silence, out of shame and hate for this empty speech. From the oral confidence to the book there lies a great distance. Here, the author deliberately chose to speak with a concern for mastery and a severity of examination unjustified by this excess of unbridled speech. However, by speaking, his goal is still to give speech to that which in him does not speak, to coerce the silence of that which wants to be silent. *Manhood* is precisely that moment of maturity in which the reign of silent intimacy, of the infant and adolescent muteness within and about oneself, is brutally ended by a demanding, explicatory and denunciatory speech. For the silent complacency which is the fault of the first age, of the innocence which means nothing and has nothing to say, *Manhood* substitutes the complacency of language, the fault which wants to recognize itself as fault and thereby recover innocence, the innocence of the fault.

Michel Leiris's book is not at all vertiginous, it refuses to abandon itself to the spontaneity of open-mouthed confidences where the deepest substance reveals itself with the irrepressible force of humors working their way out. To write this life "seen from the angle of eroticism," he tell us, he imposed some rules upon himself. He did not rely on the surge of memories nor on simple chronological succession. Like every author of autobiography, he wants to recapture his life, to "gather it up in a single solid block," but he does this by means of a view which makes order, by a preliminary clairvoyance which arranges this existence according to the profound themes it has recognized therein. These strict rules, this discipline he observes in the expression and the interpretation of himself, all of these things are what seems to him to assure the greatest chance at truth in his enterprise and also to make it the most similar to the game of bullfighting, where combat forces the instinctual threat to compose itself through a ceremonial in which nothing may be changed. The paradox of these Confessions, if it is one, therefore comes from this: the author feels that they are dangerous to him, not because of their licence or their unregulated movement, but because of the stringency of the rules he imposes upon himself to write them and the lucid objectivity he wants to attain by writing them. And there follows yet another paradox: the tone of these confidences is almost always reserved, reticent, and yet this reserve and this reticence, far from diminishing a frankness which seems as great as it possibly could be, on the contrary guarantee it and give it a character of necessity. Candor which says all says nothing but itself, and it does so perhaps by chance. But candor which is reserved to tell all also tells the reserve form which it speaks, which compels it to speak, and which makes speaking a duty by forbidding disavowal, retraction, and excuse. The "objective" tone, the vigilant, sometimes almost stuffy coldness which manifest themselves in *Manhood* respond to the subterranean "I don't want to speak," like the echo of the shyness we spoke of before, of this fundamental reticence which first of all blocks and then makes all communication insane. But, here, the vertigo has become lucidity and the dread is *sang-froid*.

Manhood is an essay of self-interpretation, in which meticulously described tastes, the randomness of conduct, all of life's anecdotal dust which is generally held to be insignificant, are related to the themes around which the profound meaning of existence is organised. This is a very different tentative from an ordinary autobiography, all the more meaningful in that it avoids the trap of causal explanations and systematic views, like that of psychoanalysis or even interpretation, and of an understanding bought at any price. There is a rare measure and mastery in this: a desire to see which does not distort the view, a power of understanding which preserves movements which are not so comprehensible, and a sense of the tragic in the human condition glimpsed through its own difficulties, without their being either exalted or abased. In *L'Aveu*, Arthur Adamov also tried to produce a confession of unquestionable pathos and sincerity, and he tried beyond this to relate his own obsessions to the situation of the world in general, such as it appears today. But he was able to pursue fully neither the one nor the other of these plans which constantly blur and interrupt one another. The very pathos of his story obliges him to restrict himself to the only pathos he cannot master and of which he only gives us brief images; and the feeling that his pain is also the pain of the world puts possibilities of facile explanation and justification into his hands, which turn him away form himself and from the rigorous and demanding view without which "the confession" perhaps remains a temptation.

The very "form" of *Manhood*, this stiffness we find in its expression, the ordered constraint which allows unleashing, the reticence which is frankness, all of these traits are not simple procedures of writing but are rather part of the existence they help to uncover. Michel Leiris explains to us that, since his fifteenth year, he has sought to project, in dress and in manners, "the English manner . . . the sober and correct style—indeed a little stiff and even funereal." And he adds: "This corresponds to a symbolic attempt at *mineralization*, a defense-reaction against my inner weakness and the scattering which threatened me; I longed for some kind of armor, seeking to achieve in my external *persona* the same idea of *rigidity* which I was pursuing poetically" (*L'Age d'homme*, 185, [127]). However, this "glacial cold," this affected impassiveness, this plaster mask were themselves chosen only out of a more profound concern and calling. The "cold" and the stone face are used as means of defense, but the "cold" is also desired for its own sake, and to these marble dreams, movements of the liveliest sensibility attach themselves. In *Aurora*, seemingly a wholly gratuitous literary work, with no other purpose than the work of language, but where, ensconced in images and symbols can be found all the themes whose vital significance is demonstrated in *Manhood*, one of the characters declares: "I must say that for me life has always been synonomous with everything soft, lukewarm, and immeasurable. Liking only the intangible, which is no part of life, I arbitrarily identified all that is cold, hard, or geometrical with this constant. . . ."[3] And this Damoclès Siriel adds: "Night and day death hung over me like a mournful threat. Perhaps, I strove to convince myself that this minerality would enable me to elude it, forming some sort of armor, and also a hiding-place away from death's shifting but infallible attacks (rather like the one insects make out of their own bodies when they feign death in order to ward off danger). Fearing death, I loathed life (since its crowning achievement is inevitably death)" (*Aurora*, 84, [90]).

We do not wish to enter into the movement of themes, into this entanglement which unites what is torn and what is beloved, what wounds and what reassures, what is held dear as both the image of death and the chance of not dying. All this belongs to the book. But we would like to show how far the ambiguity of motives deepens its meaning. Damoclès Siriel speaks to us about the threat of death which hovers over us night and day. This threat also hovers constantly over *Manhood*. But this is not a vague threat, ignorant of what it represents and oblivious to its own nature. One of the most important passages in the book seems to us to be the following: "I cannot say, strictly speaking, that *I die*, since—dying a violent death or not—I am conscious of only part of the event. And a great share of the terror which I experience at the idea of death derives perhaps from this: vertigo from remaining suspended in the middle of a seizure whose outcome I can never know because of my own unconsciousness. This kind of unreality, this *absurdity* of death, is . . . its radically terrible element" (*L'Age d'homme*,

3. Michel Leiris, *Aurora* (Paris: Gallimard, 1939, 1977), 83; *Aurora*, trans. with introduction by Anna Warby (London: Atlas, 1990), 90.

86–87, [50], translation slightly altered). We can see from these words which are so clear: the fear of dying is also the fear of not being able to die. The fact that we cannot experience the reality of death to the very end makes death unreal, and this unreality condemns us to fear that we may die only in an unreal way, not truly dying, remaining as though held, forever, between life and death, in a state of nonexistence and nondeath, from which our whole life perhaps draws its meaning and its reality. We do not know that we are dying. Nor do we know that others are dying. For the death of others remains foreign to us and always remains incomplete, because we who know of it live. We certainly do not recognize ourselves as immortal, but rather we see ourselves as condemned, in death itself, to the impossibility of dying, to the impossibility of accomplishing, of recapturing the fact of our death by abandoning ourselves to it in a sure and decisive manner.

Such a vertiginous suspension between living and dying explains, according to Michel Leiris, that in life, whatever constitutes a simulacrum of death, any loss of self, can sometimes reassure us against death and help us to stare it in the face: "If love is often conceived as a means of escaping death—or denying it or forgetting it—this is perhaps because we dimly sense that it is the only means we have for experiencing it to whatever degree, for in coitus at least we know what happens *afterwards* and can witness—albeit bitterly—the consequent disaster" (*L'Age d'homme*, 87–88, [51], translation slightly altered). But what is at stake here is not the "need to know," and we only have an indirect desire to know what happens *afterwards*. We want to be sure that death is finished, that it is a real and true whole, and this is why *afterwards* interests us, because "after death" would furnish the proof that death, though not overcome, came to pass and was accomplished once and for all. We do not want something beyond death for its own sake but rather, artificially, we want to see ourselves dead, to assure ourselves of our death by focusing upon our nothingness, from a point situated beyond death, a true gaze from beyond the tomb. By this same movement, love, insofar as, according to Michel Leiris and the traditional myths, death is lived in advance and known all the way through to its end, always fears tomorrows, its future, because it fears becoming its own awakening, this profoundly miserable moment when it discovers itself to be not finished but, on the contrary, unaccomplished in this very end. Having never been, love is the empty and interminable duration of that which nevertheless was not. And that is why love sometimes requires death for its accomplishment, as if death, itself always unfinished and incomplete when it is the death of man alone, could only truly accomplish itself by becoming the unique death of two beings already dead to themselves, so that "love stronger than death" would have this mythical meaning: love triumphs over death by putting an end to death, by making it a true end.

"Since childhood I have attributed to everything *classical* a frankly voluptuous character. Marble attracts me by its glacial temperature and its rigidity. I actually imagine myself stretched out on a slab (whose coldness I feel against my skin) or bound to a column" (*L'Age d'homme*, 56, [26]). And in *Aurora* when Damoclès Siriel makes love to alabaster figures with heads as bald as pebbles, it is said: "Thus my idea of love was always associated with this image of hardness, and ever since this time I have considered my mouth, with its cold scree of teeth, to be more than any other the organ intended for love" (*Aurora*, 84, [91]). And so, we understand that "the cold" is not a simple defensive reaction to protect a threatened intimacy against death and against others, but also as that which opens this intimacy with others, because the coldness of marble and the inviolability of stone are the privileged images whereby death and the others become confused, and also whereby death comes before its time in order to impose itself, from within this very world, in all of its monumental plenitude, removed from time's erosion. We see that the ruses of sensibility are infinite. What gets displayed to us as an effort to thwart death is already the presence of death, introduced into the heart of being, rendered beloved and desired and feeding only its own fear in order to make it more recognizable in a full and real form that alienates it from the incompleteness of life and the unreality of the "I am dying."

In *Aurora*, we read these sentences: "I have always found it more difficult than most to express myself otherwise than by using the pronoun *I*—not that this should be seen as any particular sign of pride on my part, but because for me this word *I* epitomizes the structure of the world" (*Aurora*, 39, [53]). But a bit further on, we read: "For here I have come to cathedral Death, to this third-person singular which a moment ago I crossed out with one stroke of my pen—Death, that grammatical pitchfork which imposes its ineluctable syntax on the world and myself, that rule which makes all discourse nothing but a pitiful mirage masking the nothingness of objects, whatever the words I utter and whatever this *I* which *I* put forward" (*Aurora*, 40 [54]). *Aurora* is the story of the metamorphoses by which the *I* changes itself into the *He* and the *He* tries in vain, through more and more exhausting transformations, to plunge beneath the *That* to attain a true nothing. But *Manhood* has already showed us how at the bottom of the *I* and ceaslessly uniting with it, in the very fear it inspires and the dread to which it gives rise, the *He* of death offers itself in its marble eternity and cold inviolability. In the collection of dreams entitled *Nights as Day*, on 12–13 July 1940 the following dream is recounted to us: "Waking up (with a shriek that Z . . . muffles) from the following dream: as if to catch a glimpse of something, I insert my head into an opening that resembles an oeil-de-boeuf window overlooking a dark, enclosed area akin to those cylindrical *pisé* granary lofts that I saw in Africa. . . . My anxiety derives from the fact that as I lean over this enclosed area and get a glimpse of its own inner darkness, I am actually gazing into myself."[4] *Manhood* is this lucid gaze by which the *I*, penetrating its "inner darkness," discovers that what gazes within it is no longer the *I*, "structure of the world," but already the monumental statue, with no gaze, faceless, and nameless: The *He* of sovereign Death.

—Translated by Hilari Allred

---

4. *Nuits sans Nuit et quelques jours sans jour* (Paris: Gallimard, 1961), 132; *Nights as Day, Days as Night*, trans. Richard Sieburth with a foreword by Maurice Blanchot and an introduction by Robert Shattuck (Hygiene: Eridanos, Inc., 1987), 111.

Contributors

HILARI ALLRED is a Ph.D. candidate in the Department of French at Yale University.

JEAN-CHRISTOPHE BAILLY. Essayist, poet, and writer, he is best known for his book *Marcel Duchamp*, 1984. He has also published an article "Au delà du langage: une étude sur Benjamin Peret," 1971, and a book entitled *Miro Sculpture*, 1985.

MARC BLANCHARD is Professor of French and Comparative Literature and Director of the Critical Theory Program at the University of California at Davis. His works include: *Critical Theory in the Wake of Semiotics*, *In Search of the City*, and *Trois portraits de Montaigne: essais sur la représentation à la Renaissance*.

MAURICE BLANCHOT, arguably the most influential figure in French letters, philosophy and interpretation since 1940, has published many works including essays and narratives: *L'Espace littéraire*, *Le Livre à venir*, *L'Entretien infini*, *La Part du feu*, *Michel Foucault tel que je l'imagine*, *Aminadab*, *Le très haut*, *La Folie du jour*, and *Au moment voulu*.

LYDIA DAVIS is Professor of Literature at Bard College and the author of four books of fiction: the last one, *Break it Down*, received a special citation for the PEN/Ernest Hemingway Award for Fiction. She is also the primary translator for Leiris's *Règle du jeu*.

BENJAMIN ELWOOD is a Ph.D. candidate in the Department of French at Yale University.

EDOUARD GLISSANT is Distinguished Professor of Humanities at Louisiana State University, Baton Rouge. He is the author of many works including novels (*La Lézarde*, *Le Quatrième siècle*, *La Case*

YFS 81, *On Leiris*, ed. Blanchard, © 1992 by Yale University.

du commandeur); poems (*Pays rêvé, pays réel*); plays (*Monsieur Toussaint*); and essays (*La Relation poétique, Le Discours antillais*—of which an English translation entitled *Caribbean Discourse* has recently appeared).

LEAH D. HEWITT is Associate Professor of French at Amherst College in Massachusetts. Her recently published book is entitled *Autobiographical Tightropes: Simone de Beauvoir, Nathalie Sarraute, Marguerite Duras, Monique Wittig and Maryse Condé* (University of Nebraska Press, 1990). She has also published articles on the works of Michel Leiris and Nathalie Sarraute, and on theories of autobiography. She is currently beginning a project on literature of the Occupation in France.

DENIS HOLLIER is Chairman of the Yale French Department. He has recently edited *A New History of French Literature* (Cambridge: Harvard University Press, 1989); a translation of his essay on *Georges Bataille, La Prise de la Concorde,* has recently appeared as: *Against Architecture* (Cambridge: MIT Press, 1990).

EMMANUEL LÉVINAS is Professor of Philosophy emeritus at the University of Paris. He is a specialist of hermeneutics and Judaica. His works include *Totalité et infini, Hors sujet, Sur Maurice Blanchot,* and *Quatre lectures talmudiques.*

DAVID MACEY, author of "Lacan in Context," received his doctorate from Newcastle University and works as a free-lance writer and translator.

DIDIER MALEUVRE is a Ph.D. candidate in the Department of French at Yale University working on a dissertation in nineteenth-century literature.

FRANCIS MARMANDE is a jazz critic for *Le Monde* and a lecturer at the University of Paris. He is the author of *L'Indifférence des ruines* and *Georges Bataille politique.*

CYNTHIA MESH, a Ph.D. candidate in the Department of French at Yale University, is currently writing a dissertation entitled "Language Conflict and the Francophone Caribbean Novel: An interdisciplinary Inquiry."

JEAN-LUC NANCY is Professor of Philosophy at the University of Strasbourg. He has taught at the University of California San Diego, University of California Berkeley and the Johns Hopkins University. His works include *L'Impératif catégorique, Ego sum, La Communauté désoeuvrée, L'Expérience de la liberté* and in collaboration with Philippe Lacoue-Labarthe: *L'Absolu littéraire: théorie de la littérature des romantiques allemands.* His last book translated in the United States is *The Birth to Presence.*

J. B. PONTALIS is an editor at Editions Gallimard and the author of essays on psychoanalysis including: *Après Freud, Perdre de vue.* He is coauthor with J. Laplanche of *Le Vocabulaire de la psychanalyse.*

MICHÈLE RICHMAN is Associate Professor of French at the University of Pennsylvania and the author of *Reading Georges Bataille: Beyond the Gift* (Johns Hopkins University Press, 1982). She is currently completing a study on *Anthropology and Modernism: From Durkheim to the Collège de sociologie.*

ABIGAIL S. RISCHIN, a doctoral candidate in Comparative Literature at Yale University, is currently writing a dissertation on varieties of ekphrastic experience in nineteenth-century poetry and narrative fiction.

MICHAEL SYROTINSKI is Assistant Professor of French at Illinois State University. He has published articles on Henri Thomas, Maurice Blanchot, and Jean Paulhan, and is currently preparing a critical study of Paulhan's works. His translation of Roger Caillois's *La Nécessité d'esprit* was published recently by the Lapis Press, and he is now collaborating on a translation of Paulhan's *Récits.*

BETSY WING is a novelist and free-lance translator residing in Baton Rouge, Louisiana.

The following issues are available through **Yale University Press,** Customer Service Department, 92A Yale Station, New Haven, CT 06520.

63 The Pedagogical Imperative: Teaching as a Literary Genre (1982) $15.95

64 Montaigne: Essays in Reading (1983) $15.95

65 The Language of Difference: Writing in QUEBEC(ois) (1983) $15.95

66 The Anxiety of Anticipation (1984) $15.95

67 Concepts of Closure (1984) $15.95

68 Sartre after Sartre (1985) $15.95

69 The Lesson of Paul de Man (1985) $15.95

70 Images of Power: Medieval History/Discourse/Literature (1986) $15.95

71 Men/Women of Letters: Correspondence (1986) $15.95

72 Simone de Beauvoir: Witness to a Century (1987) $15.95

73 Everyday Life (1987) $15.95

74 Phantom Proxies (1988) $15.95

75 The Politics of Tradition: Placing Women in French Literature (1988) $15.95

Special Issue: After the Age of Suspicion: The French Novel Today (1989) $15.95

76 Autour de Racine: Studies in Intertextuality (1989) $15.95

77 Reading the Archive: On Texts and Institutions (1990) $15.95

78 On Bataille (1990) $15.95

79 Literature and the Ethical Question (1991) $15.95

Special Issue: Contexts: Style and Value in Medieval Art and Literature (1991) $15.95

80 Baroque Topographies: Literature/History/Philosophy $15.95

Special subscription rates are available on a calendar year basis (2 issues per year):
Individual subscriptions $24.00   Institutional subscriptions $28.00

ORDER FORM   **Yale University Press,** 92A Yale Station, New Haven, CT 06520

Please enter my subscription for the calendar year

☐ **Special Issue (1991)**   ☐ **1991 (Nos. 79 and 80)**   ☐ **1992 (Nos. 81 and 82)**

I would like to purchase the following individual issues:

_____

_____

For individual issue, please add postage and handling:

Single issue, United States $2.75   Each additional issue $.50

Connecticut residents please add sales tax of 6%

Single issue, foreign countries $5.00   Each additional issue $1.00

Payment of $_____ is enclosed (including sales tax if applicable).

Mastercard no. _____

4-digit bank no._____Expiration date _____

VISA no._____Expiration date _____

Signature_____

SHIP TO _____

_____

_____

See the next page for ordering issues 1-59 and 61-62. Yale French Studies is also available through Xerox University Microfilms, 300 North Zeeb Road, Ann Arbor, MI 48106.

The following issues are still available through the **Yale French Studies Office,** 2504A Yale Station, New Haven, CT 06520.

19/20 Contemporary Art $3.50	44 Paul Valéry $5.00	Decor $6.00
23 Humor $3.50	45 Language as Action $5.00	58 In Memory of Jacques Ehrmann $6.00
33 Shakespeare $3.50	46 From Stage to Street $3.50	59 Rethinking History $6.00
35 Sade $3.50	47 Image & Symbol in the Renaissance $3.50	60 Cinema/Sound $6.00
38 The Classical Line $3.50	49 Science, Language, & the Perspective Mind $3.50	61 Toward a Theory of Description $6.00
39 Literature and Revolution $3.50	50 Intoxication and Literature $3.50	62 Feminist Readings: French Texts/American Contexts $6.00
41 Game, Play, Literature $5.00	53 African Literature $3.50	
42 Zola $5.00	54 Mallarmé $5.00	
43 The Child's Part $5.00	57 Locus: Space, Landscape,	

Add for postage & handling

Single issue, United States $1.75   Each additional issue $.50
Single issue, foreign countries $2.50   Each additional issue $1.50

YALE FRENCH STUDIES, 2504A Yale Station, New Haven, Connecticut 06520
A check made payable to YFS is enclosed. Please send me the following issue(s):

Issue no.   Title   Price

_____

_____

Postage & handling   _____

Total   _____

Name _____

Number/Street _____

City_____ State _____ Zip_____

The following issues are now available through Kraus Reprint Company, Route 100, Millwood, N. Y. 10546.

1 Critical Bibliography of Existentialism	17 The Art of the Cinema
2 Modern Poets	18 Passion & the Intellect, or Malraux
3 Criticism & Creation	21 Poetry Since the Liberation
4 Literature & Ideas	22 French Education
5 The Modern Theatre	24 Midnight Novelists
6 France and World Literature	25 Albert Camus
7 André Gide	26 The Myth of Napoleon
8 What's Novel in the Novel	27 Women Writers
9 Symbolism	28 Rousseau
10 French-American Literature Relationships	29 The New Dramatists
11 Eros, Variations...	30 Sartre
12 God & the Writer	31 Surrealism
13 Romanticism Revisited	32 Paris in Literature
14 Motley: Today's French Theater	34 Proust
15 Social & Political France	48 French Freud
16 Foray through Existentialism	51 Approaches to Medieval Romance

36/37 Structuralism has been reprinted by Doubleday as an Anchor Book.
55/56 Literature and Psychoanalysis has been reprinted by Johns Hopkins University Press, and can be ordered through Customer Service, Johns Hopkins University Press, Baltimore, MD 21218.

NOVITÀ - NEW BOOK

ATHANOR

Rivista di arti visive, letteratura, semiotica, filosofia
Diretta da Augusto Ponzio e Claude Gandelman
Numeri monografici. Periodicità annuale

N. 1, 1990

IL SENSO E L'OPERA

Coordinamento: Istituto di Filosofia del Linguaggio, Facoltà di Lingue
Via Garruba 6, 70124 Bari - Italia, tel. (080) 317460

Amministrazione e abbonamenti
A. Longo Editore, via Paolo Costa 33, 48100 Ravenna, tel. 0544/27026
Ogni volume: per l'Italia L. 25.000, per l'Estero L. 35.000
I pagamenti vanno effettuati anticipatamente o con vaglia postale o con
versamento su ccp nr. 14226484 intestato a Edizioni Longo.

COMING IN APRIL

"One of the central works of what we may call modernity."
— Richard Howard, from the Translator's Note

MANHOOD
A Journey from Childhood into the
Fierce Order of Virility
Michel Leiris
Translated by Richard Howard
With a Foreword by Susan Sontag

- "Not only one of the frankest of autobiographies, but also a brilliantly written book, Leiris' *Manhood* mingles memories, philosophic refections, sexual revelation, meditations on bullfighting, and the life-long progress of self-discovery. "
  — *Washington Post Book World*

- "Leiris writes to appall, and thereby to receive from his readers the gift of a strong emotion–the emotion needed to defend himself against the indignation and disgust he expects to arouse in his readers." — Susan Sontag, *New York Review of Books*

- "As an autobiographer Leiris lends his attention to language as much as to life, concentrating on certain salient words or groups of words in the certainty that these will show themselves to be priveleged points of entry into his past. . . . Leiris began writing about himself to try to rationalize certain, as he believed, crippling weaknesses in his personality. The books were intended to have a practical result, which was to cure him of particularly tenacious inhibitions by making a public spectacle of their etiology." — John Sturrock, *New Literary History*

Paper $12.95

THE UNIVERSITY OF CHICAGO PRESS
5801 South Ellis Chicago, IL 60637